The Diversity of Crop Plants

The Diversity of Crop Plants

J. G. HAWKES

HARVARD UNIVERSITY PRESS

Cambridge, Massachusetts

London, England

1983

Library of Congress Cataloging in Publication Data

Hawkes, J. G. (John Gregory)
    The diversity of crop plants.

    "Based on the John M. Prather lectures in biology . . .
    Harvard University . . . April 1977" — P.
    Includes bibliographical references and index.
    1. Field crops — Varieties.   2. Field crops — Evolution.
3. Field crops — Germplasm resources.   4. Plants, Cultivated — Varieties.   5. Plants, Cultivated — Evolution.
6. Plants, Cultivated — Germplasm resources.   I. Title.
SB185.75.H38   1983   631.5′2   82-23253
ISBN 0-674-21286-X

Preface

We live at a time when recurrent world problems of famine and malnutrition have forced plant breeders and agronomists to focus their attention more than ever before on breeding for increased quantity and quality of food production. Even urban dwellers are beginning to take more than a passing interest in how yields can be improved and the hungry fed. The benefits derived from the production of animal protein must be balanced against those of the less wasteful production of plant protein, which, however, is not necessarily so palatable. World population growth continues exponentially, but the land available for agriculture is finite, and we are already perilously near its limits. Hence, to make the best possible use of our plant resources, we need to improve crop yields and quality by plant breeding and by other means.

One approach to this problem is to attempt to clarify our ideas on the nature of cultivated plants and the processes by which they came into existence. How did early man, some 10,000 years ago, in what has been called the Neolithic Revolution, begin the process of converting an apparently unpromising group of weedy-looking wild plants into the successful crops we know today? This is not a subject of theoretical interest only. A knowledge of the genetic variability of crop plants and the processes by which they have been converted from wild species into cultivated ones, together with

knowledge of the evolutionary relationships of the wild and cultivated species, has proved to be of considerable value to plant
breeders in providing a better understanding of the material with
which they work. Much of this information comes from interdisci-
plinary research conducted by the population geneticist, the agro-
ecologist, the physiologist, the taxonomist, and indeed the archae-
ologist and ethnobotanist, all of whom can throw light on the
origins and evolution of crop plants.

It is particularly unfortunate that just when we need it most the
ancient genetic diversity of our crop plants and related wild species
is under the greatest threat of destruction. This genetic diversity is
urgently required as a basic source for breeding new higher-yield-
ing, more resistant, and better-adapted varieties in an attempt to
relieve worldwide malnutrition and hunger.

In this book I have examined the ways in which cultivated plants
have evolved and diversified, the importance of this diversity, and
the means by which it can be conserved and made available to
breeders throughout the world. I hope that the book will be of value
not only to plant breeders themselves but also to students of evolution and of biosystematics. Cultivated plants have generally been
neglected by taxonomists. Yet they have been of great importance
to students of evolution. Indeed, Darwin himself was the first to
point out their value as organisms that had undergone rapid evolution during a comparatively short period of time and under strong
artificial selection pressures.

The origins and evolution of cultivated plants are fascinating and
intellectually exciting subjects; at the same time they are of strong
practical importance. I shall be well content if I have managed in
this book to convey some of this excitement to the reader.

This book is based on the John M. Prather Lectures in Biology,
which I gave at Harvard University in April 1977, through the kind
invitation of the chairman of the 1977 Prather committee, Professor
Otto Solbrig. I should like to take this opportunity to thank the
committee, and other members of Harvard University, for their kind
and friendly hospitality during the period of the lectureship.

Contents

The Nature of Cultivated Plants

There have probably been very few human societies in which plants did not play a major dietary role. Man may have existed as a species for a period of one or two million years, according to how one defines him. During that whole period, and long before, when our ancestors were still apes, they gathered wild plants in the form of seeds, roots, juicy stems, and fruits, together with whatever animals that they could catch or trap as well, by hunting and fishing. This was the so-called hunter-gatherer stage of our cultural prehistory, though the hunting phase was probably not always present in every society. At some time in the late Mesolithic period or the early Neolithic Age, varying according to the area under consideration, humans began to domesticate plants. Thus agriculture, which seems to us now to be so basic to our existence as a species, is in fact a very recent phenomenon in our socioeconomic development, having originated only 10,000 years ago, or even more recently.

It is now generally supposed that agriculture began not once but several times, more or less simultaneously and in different regions of the world. It may have taken place first in the Fertile Crescent of the Near East (see Fig. 1.1), where wheat, barley, and certain pulses were domesticated. There was also an independent center of domestication in northern China, based on millets (see Fig. 1.2), and still another in Meso-America, where squashes, beans, peppers, and

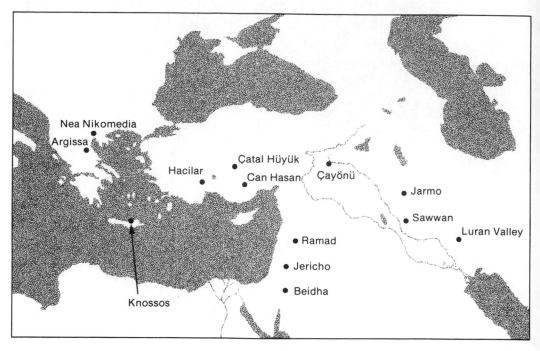

Fig. 1.1   The Fertile Crescent, showing the main 7th and 6th millennia B.C.
sites in the Near East and Greece from which plant remains have
been examined. (Adapted from Zohary, 1973; reprinted by permission of Keter Publishing House, Jerusalem.)

maize were domesticated (see Fig. 1.3). There is now strong evidence for a fourth independent invention of agriculture in the
South American Andes (south-central Peru) (see Fig. 1.4). The
archaeological evidence, based on food remains, strongly suggests
that agriculture developed independently in these four nuclear
areas. Some other areas have also been postulated, such as one in
Southeast Asia (Sauer, 1952), but the archaeological evidence for
them is scanty at present. In any case, in the period between 7,000
and 10,000 years ago our ancestors began to adopt farming and a
settled mode of existence. Indeed, many authorities think that a settled existence was a prerequisite for the invention of agriculture.

    This invention, if that is what it was, for some believe it to have
been a process much less conscious than that, was a revolution in
man's development as important as his discovery of fire and the
wheel. In many ways it was more revolutionary than the technolog-

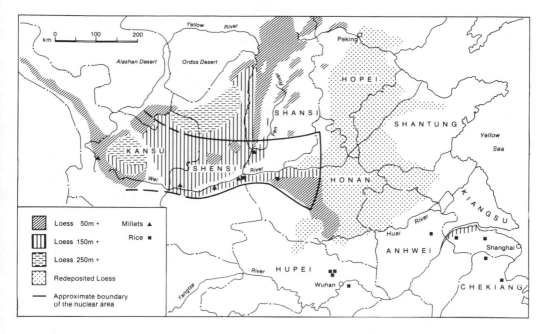

Fig. 1.2 Northern China, showing the early centers of domestication of millet and rice on the loess soils, about 7000 B.P. or earlier (rice later, about 5000 B.P.). (Ping-Ti Ho, 1969.)

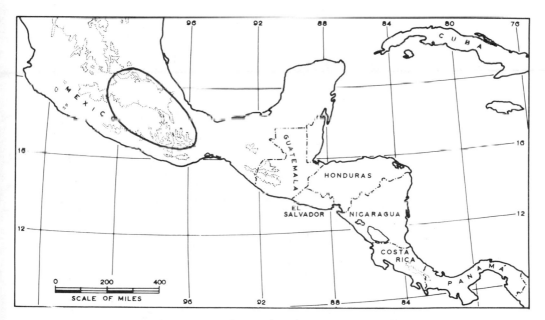

Fig. 1.3 Presumed nuclear center of agricultural origins in Meso-America.

Fig. 1.4 Central to Southern Peru. Presumed nuclear center of agricultural origins in South America.

ical advances of a few centuries ago. Gordon Childe (1936) termed it, in fact, the Neolithic Revolution — an emotive phrase leading us to suppose that it took place in the space of a few weeks. Several hundred to even a thousand years are probably nearer the mark, but on a geological time scale this is a very short period indeed.

Whatever the length of the Neolithic Revolution, there is no doubt that man's life and activities were revolutionized by agriculture. While cultivated plants have been molded and changed by man, because they are as much a part of material culture as tools, weapons, clothes, and dwellings, the plants in their turn have changed man. Agriculture has enabled man to abandon his nomadic lifestyle and settle down in one place to build permanent dwellings, and to relate himself to the rhythms of the seasons and the cycles of the sun and moon. He learned the correct period to till the soil, to sow and to harvest, to reserve seeds from the harvest for the next year's sowing, and to learn the uses of plants.

Over time, with adequate food and leisure, our ancestors could develop their artistic talents and primitive searchings toward science and technology. In hunting and gathering communities, always on the move and always searching for food, this would have been impossible, except where food was very abundant. Even so, a number of writers, such as J.R. Harlan (1975c, chapter 1), have pointed out that leisure and artistic activities, along with a degree of happiness and relaxation not known to farming people, are found in nonagricultural societies. It is, of course, well known that certain peoples in the far north (Esquimos, for example) and in the tropics (tribes in New Guinea or Australia, for instance) have never adopted farming, even though at least in the tropics it would have been quite possible. People there appear to be content, but it must be pointed out that population numbers are small. There is no doubt whatsoever that, in general, a more certain and abundant food supply is normally available to societies having an agricultural economy, so that a golden age of happy nomadic gatherers is perhaps more imagined than real.

For all the enormous impact that cultivated plants have made on us, it comes as something of a shock, therefore, to realize that of the approximately 200,000 species of flowering plants in existence, only about 3,000 species have been used for food, even though most have probably been sampled at one time or another, often, perhaps, with disastrous consequences. Possibly only about 200 species have been domesticated as crops, and only some 15 to 20 are now crops of major importance (Heiser, 1973, chapter 5; National Academy of Sciences, 1975).

There are both qualitative and quantitative differences between cultivated and wild plants also. Recently cultivated plants, such as rubber trees (*Hevea*) and subterranean clover (*Trifolium subterraneum*) differ hardly at all from their related wild forms, except, perhaps, for some ecotypic differences. Cultigens that were domesticated thousands of years ago, such as wheat, maize, and potatoes, are very far removed morphologically and physiologically from those wild species that we believe to be their ancestors. Many of these, such as wheat, tobacco, potatoes, and bananas, have evolved through complex processes of hybridization after their initial domestication and can no longer be considered the same species as their wild or primitive cultivated ancestral forms.

Crop plants have been exploited for a variety of purposes. As food, seeds, fruits, roots, and tubers have supplied the starches, and sweet juicy stems and fruits the sugars, necessary for basic energy; certain seeds have been sources of protein and others of oils and fats used in cooking. Plants and plant products have had a host of other uses in clothing, dyes, condiments, stimulants, vitamins, medicines, and even poisons. Very often, plants have had several different uses. Thus, flax and cotton provide both fiber and oil; peanuts and sunflower seeds produce proteins and oil. Lettuce and brassicas, which include cabbages and turnips, were probably first domesticated for their seed oils and only later were used as vegetables; maize was and is primarily a source of carbohydrates but now also provides oil from the embryos, and poppies, once used for oil, are now a drug source. According to Smartt (1976), this development of multipurposed crops results in the persistence of the most versatile ones, those able to respond to different types of selection. In his view, versatility of a crop plant thus ensures its survival.

In a general way, cultivated plants respond to the same processes of natural selection as wild ones. This selection acts on the variation derived from gene mutations and recombinations. However, in addition to the natural selection pressures to which wild plants are exposed, cultivated plants also face artificial selection by man, which in some instances is of greater importance in effecting rapid change than natural selection. Much artificial selection was, and perhaps still is, "unconscious selection" (Darwin, 1868, chapter 20), in which man acts without any awareness of his role as an agent of selection. Darlington (1973) points out that this should really be classed as natural selection; even so, because man is the causal agent, it has become customary to speak of this as a type of artificial selection.

Special Characteristics of Cultivated Plants

When we compare the domesticated forms of cultivated plants with their wild prototypes, certain trends in domestication are evident. Although these trends are not all developed to an equal extent in every cultigen, their presence in unrelated species clearly reveals the results of similar selection pressures and promotes an understanding of those processes. Schwanitz (1967, pp. 136 ff.) points out that many undesirable characters, such as spines, prickles, and alkaloids, can still be found in the cultigens, but in general the disappearance of "wild type" characters is very striking. The characters of greatest interest in this respect are as follows:

Reduced competitiveness with other species

One of the characteristics of cultivated plants and their wild ancestors is an inability to compete successfully with natural climax vegetation, and a marked preference for open, disturbed, or ruderal habitats with bare soil and a minimum of competition with other species. They are thus spoken of as ecological weeds, rather than horticultural weeds (Grant, 1967). Bunting (1960) and Harlan and de Wet (1965) have thoroughly analyzed the two definitions of weed. The general, or horticultural, definition is of a noxious or unwanted plant that should be rooted out, depending of course on where it grows. Thus, grass is a weed in a flower bed but not a weed in a lawn. The ecological definition of a weed is a plant of secondary successions, that is, one establishing itself and growing quickly on bare soil, almost regardless of the nutritional status of that soil, but dying out rapidly when the soil becomes covered by perennial grasses, herbs, shrubs, and trees. Often, but not always, weeds require high levels of nitrogen in the soil.

Both the ancestors of cultivated plants and the crops themselves possess this "weediness," which is a key feature in domestication, as I will show in Chapter 2. However, the wild species are more aggressive, more able to establish themselves quickly than are the cultivated species to which they have given rise. Cultivated plants have thus almost or entirely lost the ability to grow by their own efforts in natural vegetation, while their wild prototypes must clearly have been able to do so, even though they needed rather special conditions.

Of course "escapes" of cultivated plants back to the wild sometimes occur, especially when cultigens that were only recently domesticated move into habitats that are fairly similar to those of the natural species. Thus, the tetraploid potato, *Solanum tuberosum*, escapes now and again in the Andes and in the coastal regions of Chile, where it seems to be able to reestablish itself as a weed, bordering fields or even growing on the seashore – both habitats where competition with the natural vegetation is considerably reduced. Other "escapes" from cultivation are better explained as weed-crop complexes. For instance, the weedy ancestors of hemp in central Asia and rye in southwestern Asia can hardly be distinguished from the crops themselves, since they form part of the same gene pool, frequently hybridizing, and belonging to the same biological, if not taxonomic, species. These are kept apart only by human disruptive selection. On the whole, however, cultigens do not become established as escapes in wild vegetation, because they have been subjected to artificial selection processes that have reduced their ability to compete with other species, though of course the individuals of any one species must retain the ability to compete with each other when grown in fairly dense rows.

Gigantism

Gigantism is a phenomenon that in general refers only to the part of the plant of interest to man, though pleiotropic effects often cause gigantism in other parts as well. For instance, the stem and leaves of the sunflower are also oversized, even though the flower is the part man has emphasized through selection (Heiser, 1955). Man has similarly selected large fruits, seeds, tubers, rhizomes, and so forth, according the the part he wished to use (see Fig 1.5). In *Brassica oleracea*, processes of selection for large leaves in headed cabbages, larges inflorescences in cauliflowers, large stems in the mar-

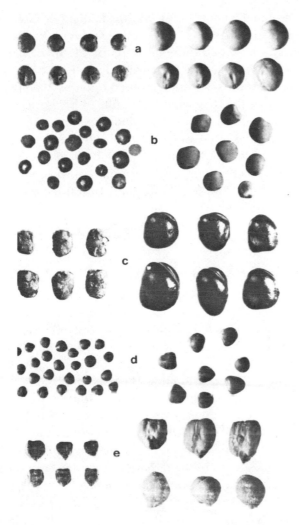

Fig. 1.5 Differences in size between ancient (*left*) and recent (*right*) seeds of five cultivated pulses. (*a*) Pea, *Pisum sativum* L., carbonized seed from Early Bronze Age, Arad, Israel. (*b*) Lentil, *Lens culinaris* Medik., carbonized remains from Late Bronze Age, Manole, Bulgaria. (*c*) Broad bean, *Vicia faba* L., carbonized seed from Copper Age, Chibanes, Portugal. (*d*) Bitter vetch, *Vicia ervilia* (L.) Willd., remains from Late Bronze Age, Manole, Bulgaria. (*e*) Chickpea, *Cicer arietinum* L., carbonized seed from Early Bronze Age, Arad, Israel. Magnification about 1.8. (From Zohary and Hopf, 1973; copyright 1973 by the American Association for the Advancement of Science.)

rowstem kales, large numbers of leaves in all kales, or large axillary buds in brussels sprouts bear witness to the marvelous genetic plasticity of this species when different parts of the plant have been selected for man's benefit. The large-fruited apples and pears of the Caucasus and central Asia were remarked upon by Vavilov (1930), who wondered whether they were the results of heterosis, or hybrid vigor. This seems doubtful, however, and one supposes that early man initially became interested in large-fruited and large-seeded variants merely because of their size, which he then selected for "consciously," or "methodically," as Darwin termed it. One should not, however, rule out the possibility that natural hybridization of species or subspecies provided a range of recombinants from which large forms of the plant organ of interest to man were then artificially selected.

Wide range of morphological variability

Large numbers, indeed, several tens of thousands, of cultivars of wheat, maize, rice, barley, and other crops are known, the variations among them largely being characterized morphologically. Again, Darwin (1868) was the first to point out that morphological variability, as well as gigantism, was to be found in those organs or parts of the plant of interest to man. Thus, one finds a tremendous range of tuber shape, color, and patterning in South American potatoes and little in their flowers and leaves, contrasted with the almost uniform tubers of all wild species of potatoes. One also finds a vast range of fruit shape, size, and color in *Capsicum* peppers (Fig. 1.6) and in tomatoes, despite the rather uniform flowers, contrasted with the poor variation of the fruits in wild species. Further, one can see the wide range of fruit types in cultivated *Cucurbits* (squashes, pumpkins, marrows, gourds) and in *Lagenaria* (bottle gourd) contrasted with the uniform wild species (Fig. 1.7), and the many kinds of spikes in wheats and barleys, contrasted with the uniform spikes of the wild types.

Is this explosion of variation the result of natural or unconscious selection? Perhaps in part. Brightly colored potato tubers are easier to see in the soil than are the dull, brownish ones of wild species and may thus be collected more frequently. However, this "visibility factor" really accounts for only the bright colors of selected mutants, not for their bizarre patternings, shapes, and color combina-

Fig. 1.6 Variability of fruit size, shape, and color in *Caspicum* (chili pepper). (Photo: Dr. Barbara Pickersgill.)

tions. High visibility may perhaps also be used as an argument for selection of some pepper and tomato fruits, but it can hardly be applied to the selection of the colors of the kernels of maize.

Here I should like to introduce a completely new concept of selection, which I call "aesthetic selection." We must remember that our early ancestors designed and decorated basketry, pottery, weaving, metalwork, bone and stone carvings, bark paintings, and many other objects. I believe that we should also credit them with taking pleasure in selecting interesting colors and shapes of mutants of pepper, gourd, and tomato fruits, and the colors of potato tubers and maize grains as well. Domesticated plants are partly creations of human beings, who, through selection, have made aesthetic masterpieces of crops. The trend to select beautiful variants

Fig. 1.7 Variation in fruit characters in collections of *Lagenaria siceraria* from northeastern Brazil. (Collection: Dr. Barbara Pickersgill. Photo: Dr. Charles Heiser.)

seems to be particularly prevalent in New World cultivated plants, but is this owing to the plants or to the peoples? One is inclined to believe that probably both are responsible, but the matter obviously needs further thought and some experimentation – this could be a fascinating line of inquiry for ethnologists.

Wide range of physiological adaptation

In his wanderings, man has taken domesticated plants far from the regions where they had grown wild, and natural selection pressures of soil and climate have caused their adaptation to conditions very different from those in their original homes. In addition, there is evidence that in the new regions, crop plants were brought into contact with related species with which they exchanged genes and picked up new types of adaptation. This may have taken place through polyploidy, as in the wheats and potatoes, though it may also have occurred at the diploid level, as in rice, rye, lentil, sorghum, and tomato.

Artificial selection, no doubt, has also played a role in the physiological adaptations of crops to new environments. For instance the early-maturing forms of wheats and barleys in Ethiopia mentioned by Vavilov (1926) developed because of the particular farming practices there; cattle are allowed onto the fields rather early in the season, so only those varieties that mature early are harvested. Furthermore, as Bennett, quoting from Vavilov's works, pointed out (1971), several thousands of such agroecotypes of wheats and other cereals are known. "A flood of evolution has been released by cultivation" in which the agriculture of weedy domesticates grown In small plots has provided a living laboratory of evolution that has continued almost up to the present day. Indeed, it still continues in those crops which are not yet considered "important" by those who judge crops in terms of thousands of hectares, but which are grown on small-scale farms and in kitchen gardens, where a mixture of crops and weeds still provides opportunities for continuing evolutionary change.

Suppression of natural mechanisms for distribution

In all domesticates, the natural means by which the plant is distributed have been suppressed. For example, wild grasses and cereals (such as *Triticum boeoticum, Hordeum spontaneum,* and *Zea mexicana*) have a brittle, or "shattering," rachis that breaks easily to distribute the spikelets or florets after the grains have matured. Mutations leading to nonbrittle rachises take place in wild grasses (Harlan et al., 1973) but are selected against because of the inability of the plants to disseminate their seeds or grains. Domesticated cereals, however, such as *T. aestivum, H. sativum,* and *Z. mays,* have developed a nonbrittle rachis: under cultivation, the nonshattering character is at a selective advantage. Intermediate forms having semibrittle rachises, such as *T. monococcum* and *T. spelta,* also exist. Generally, development of nonbrittle rachises is controlled by a recessive allele at one or sometimes at two loci, but more complex genetic situations occasionally occur.

Wild grasses and cereals, in addition to brittle rachises, possess awns, the bristlelike processes on the tips of the lemmas, generally thought to aid in grain distribution. They have been reduced or eliminated in many varieties or bread wheat, rice, and oats but still exist in most primitive cultivars (Fig. 1.8). In fact, they are now considered important assimilating organs of the grain during the late phase of ripening and are even claimed to protect the grains from bird damage (Dadayin, personal communication); hence, breeders are now breeding awns back into the advanced cultivars.

There are many other examples of suppressed distribution mechanisms. In wild legumes (*Phaseolus vulgaris* subsp. *aborigineus*, for example; Fig. 1.9) a thick parchment layer in the pods dries and twists until the seeds are released explosively, but in cultivated forms (*P. vulgaris* subsp. *vulgaris*; Fig. 1.10), the layer is very thin and apparently has no function. Some wild and weedy plants, such as the opium poppy, have open pores for seed distribution, but their cultivated forms have pores that are completely closed (Fig. 1.11). Long, wandering stolons of wild potatoes have been replaced by very short ones in the cultivated species, and a suppression of the intercalary meristems in cultivated peanuts results in a grouping of the capsules at the base of the plant, rather than one or two meters away, as they are in wild species.

Such changes in plants have evolved in response to man's needs to gather easily the products that interest him. Thus if the cereal rachis breaks, the grains are lost; if the legume seeds or poppy seeds are dispersed, they cannot be collected for resowing the following year; and if the potato stolons or peanut meristems are long, the tubers or seeds, as the case may be, cannot be found. Such selection can be largely unconscious, as these examples clearly indicate. Archaeological evidence (see Kaplan, 1965) indicates that these processes of selection took place very early in the history of the domestication of each crop. In fact, archaeologists use the processes to identify the cultigens, so one has to be careful of circular arguments.

Suppression of protective mechanisms

Plants have evolved protective mechanisms to prevent the destruction of certain organs from those predators which do not perform a useful function in the distribution of propagules, that is, parts of the plant such as seeds, tubers, and so forth that are distrib-

Fig. 1.8 Wild, weed, and cultivated oats; spikelets and florets. *Top*: diploid wild species; *middle*: tetraploid wild species, and primitive cultivated species; *bottom*: hexaploids (from left to right): wild, cultivated, wild, cultivated. The wild and primitive cultivated species all have awns; the advanced cultivated species lack them. (Bell, 1965.)

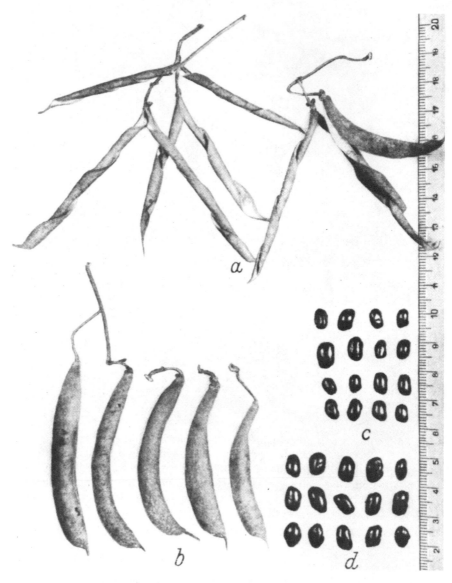

Fig. 1.9 The presumed wild prototype of the common bean (*Phaseolus vulgaris* subsp. *aborigineus* Burk.) with shattering explosive pods: (*a*) dehisced pods, (*b*) undehisced pods, and (*c* and *d*) two seed variants. (Burkart and Brücher, 1953.)

Fig. 1.10   The common bean, *Phaseolus vulgaris* L., showing the pods which split open easily and have no explosive mechanism for dispersing the seeds.

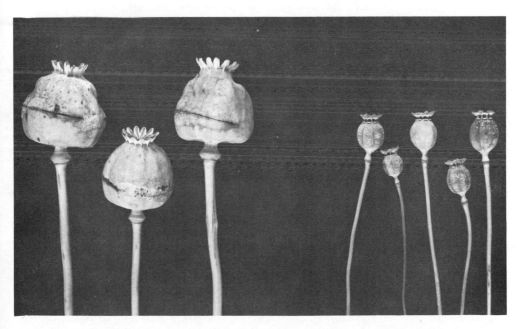

Fig. 1.11   Opium poppy (*Papaver somniferum* L.). Wild forms with smaller fruits and well-developed pores for seed dispersal. Cultivated forms with larger fruits and closed pores to prevent loss of seeds. Note scars where latex has been removed for opium production.

uted. Thus the cultivated cucurbits possess a sweet flesh, while the wild ones have a bitter flesh, unpalatable to mammals but presumably well liked by birds, who act as seed distributors. The shallow-rooted yams are bitter, to prevent their being eaten by burrowing mammals, but man has selected sweet cultivars. On the other hand, the deep-rooting yams are protected by the depths at which they grow and are sweet-fleshed, because the protective bitter flesh is unnecessary, but in this case man has selected shallow-rooted cultivars. Spines in fruit trees such as apples, plums, pears, and citrus have been totally or partially suppressed, as have the thorns on egg-plants (aubergines; Figs. 1.12, 1.13). The better yielding cassavas are still very poisonous, however, and need special grating and pressing out of the juice before they can be eaten. These examples demonstrate, then, that people have tended to select plants for features suiting their needs and have not in every case taken the trouble to eliminate totally those features, such spines, that they do *not* prefer.

Reduction of seed fertility in vegetatively reproducing crops

Some scientists have asserted that vegetative reproduction causes sterility. This is rather doubtful, and it would probably be truer to say that selection of mutants for yield and vigor of the roots or tubers has resulted in the elimination of fertility. The metabolites that would have gone to nourish the fruits and seeds have thus been diverted to the vegetative storage organs. High- and often odd-numbered polyploids, and a multitude of cytotypes that would have been quickly eliminated by the sieve of sexual reproduction, are often seen in vegetatively reproducing crops such as yams and sugar cane. This condition generally results in sterility through breakdown of the mechanisms of chromosomal pairing. However, genetic sterility is also evident in diploids such as *Curcuma* (Prana, 1977) or tetraploids such as *Solanum tuberosum*, where meiotic irregularities still occur despite the euploid numbers, and where seed production is very low or even completely absent (Swaminathan, 1954).

Change of habit

Cultivated plants frequently differ from their wild relatives in their habit and forms of growth. For example, the long stems and

Fig. 1.12 Wild African eggplant (*Solanum dasyphyllum* Schum. and Thonn.) from Togo. Note the thorny stem, leaves, and calyx. (Photo: R. N. Lester.)

Fig. 1.13. Cultivated African eggplant (*S. macrocarpon* L.) from Togo. Note complete absence of thorns on all parts of the plant. The leaves are eaten as spinach and the fruits of both wild and cultivated species are sometimes cooked in stews. Although each has been given a separate species name, it seems certain that *S. macrocarpon* was derived through human selection from *S. dasyphyllum* and is really conspecific with it. (Photo: R. N. Lester.)

vigorous branching, with indeterminate growth, of the wild species of *Phaseolus* (Smartt, 1969: in Ucko and Dimbleby, 1976), sunflower (Heiser, 1955), sorghum (Harlan et al., 1973), and *Ipomoea batatas* (Yen, 1967) are reduced to the relatively unbranched stem type with a limited node number in the cultivars. It is clearly easier for man to manipulate plants of this type for cultivation in a garden or a field. The ultimate stages of stem reduction are found in such plants as the dwarf tomatoes and dwarf courgettes (*Cucurbita pepo*), which have been tailored to the requirements of horticulture in a small garden plot.

Another such change during domestication is the trend for perennials to become annuals. Very often the change to an annual habit has already taken place before domestication begins, as it did in rice and maize, but this is not always so. In certain root crops, such as carrots, parsnips, and turnips, the biennial habit has been converted into an annual one so that the food store set aside by the plant for flowering during the next season can be used in the same season by man.

Rapid, even germination

There is an advantage for a wild species to possess seeds of different dormancy periods that germinate unevenly. In this way it can ensure that some of its seeds will survive if conditions for germination in a particular season prove to be unfavorable. However, this is an unsuitable character for field-scale cultivation, and the trait has been bred out of all annual crops, where even and rapid germination are required to ensure a uniformly harvestable product.

Inbreeding mechanisms

Many wild species of plants are outbreeders, and apparently most of the ancestors of our annual crops were too. However, in many crops — wheat, barley, and tomatoes, for instance — outbreeding has been replaced by inbreeding. Nevertheless, there are some notable exceptions, such as maize and rye. In the inbreeders, variation has been replaced by uniformity, or near uniformity, which is clearly an advantage for large-scale field cultivation. Even so, uniformity can also be attained at a satisfactory level in outbreeders.

From these descriptions of the special characteristics of cultivated plants, we can see the effects of a syndrome, or a complex of selective processes, that is to a large extent common to our field crops and that can also be observed in fruit trees and even in ornamentals. These are the processes that direct the evolution of plants under domestication and are considerably different from those that direct the evolution of purely wild species. There are, of course, many mechanisms of natural selection that act upon wild and cultivated plants alike, but as my purpose has been to point out the less-obvious differences, I have not felt it necessary to mention these common selective pressures.

Polyploidy in Cultivated Plants

About 40% of all species of flowering plants are polyploids (Solbrig, 1970), and one would therefore expect to find the same phenomenon occurring quite frequently in crop plants also. Indeed, it is often stated that polyploidy occurs more frequently in cultivated than it does in wild species.

As Table 1.1 shows, many crops have remained constantly diploid, while others have developed polyploid series that are often of considerable complexity. Wheat exhibits one of the classic polyploid series, which was recognized as early as 1918 by Sakamura in Japan. Oats also show a complex polyploid situation, which is not well understood and contains at least two polyploid series. On the other hand, four of the major cereals of the world — barley, rye, maize, and rice — are uncompromisingly diploid, even though polyploids are found in other sections of some of these genera that are not closely related to the cereals. For the most part, the vegeta-

Table 1.1 Levels of ploidy in certain widely grown species of field and tree crops.

DIPLOIDS	POLYPLOIDS
Almond	Apple $(2\times, 3\times)$
Barley	Bananas $(2\times, 3\times, 4\times)$
Cabbage	Canna $(2\times, 3\times)$
Chickpea	Cassava $(4\times)$
Cocoa	Cherries $(2\times, 4\times)$
Coconut	Coffee $(2\times, 4\times)$
Cocoyam	Cotton $(2\times, 4\times)$
Coix	Curcuma $(2\times, 3\times)$
Ginger	Oats $(2\times, 4\times, 6\times)$
Lentil	Peanut $(4\times)$
Maize	Pear $(2\times, 3\times)$
Oil palm	Plums $(2\times, 4\times, 6\times)$
Olive	Potatoes $(2\times, 3\times, 4\times, 5\times)$
Peach	Rose $(2\times, 3\times, 4\times, 5\times, 6\times)$
Phaseolus beans	Sugar cane (variable)
Pineapple	Sweet potato $(4\times)$
Rice	Taro $(2\times, 3\times)$
Rye	Tobacco $(4\times)$
Tea	Wheat $(2\times, 4\times, 6\times)$
Tomato	Yams (variable)

tively propagated crops, such as potatoes, yams, sweet potato, cassava, curcuma, taro, canna, bananas, and sugar cane are polyploids. This would be expected, if chromosomal sterility that was not eliminated by the sieve of sexual selection was allowed to build up in the vegetatively propagated material. Nevertheless, other vegetatively propagated crops such as cocoyam (*Xanthosoma*), ginger, and pineapple seem to be completely diploid.

Pickersgill and Heiser (1976) have pointed out that few crops reproduce entirely asexually; most of them produce seedlings from sexual reproduction now and again, thus adding to the variation in the crop if the seedlings are allowed to survive. Plant breeders also need to use this method of sexual reproduction. Nevertheless, many cultivars of potatoes, sweet potatoes, curcuma, and bananas are entirely sterile, and breeders must then return to the more "primitive" forms of these plants, which are not completely sterile, before seed can be obtained. Sexual reproduction in most vegetatively propagated crops is predominantly outbreeding; this maintains heterozygosity and releases considerable diversity when crosses do occur.

The phenomenon of a multitude of cytotypes (that is, chromosome numbers) and some very high chromosome numbers in yams (*Dioscorea*) and sugar cane has yet to be assessed, because other crops similar to yams — sweet potatoes, for instance — seem to manage quite well at only the tetraploid level. Yet in both yams and sugar cane, one can distinguish an underlying basis of simple polyploidy that has been overlaid in part by the complexity of artificial hybridization. Thus the base number in yams is $x = 9$ or 10, and most species seem to be basically tetraploid ($2n = 36$ or 40), with cytotypes ranging up to 100, or even 144, somatic chromosomes. In sugar cane the base number is $x = 10$ or 12; *Saccharum officinarum* seems to be octoploid, with $2n = 8x = 80$, and many forms show 40 bivalents at meiosis. *S. robustum*, the presumed wild prototype, seems to occur as a hexaploid ($2n = 60$) *and* as an octoploid ($2n = 80$), but in both species somatic numbers up to 124, or even 180, seem to occur. Of course, plants with such high numbers are sterile.

A number of the vegetatively propagated crops, such as turmeric (*Curcuma*), taro (*Colocasia*), and canna, possess triploid cytotypes in addition to diploids. Many species of wild potato that are mainly diploid exhibit the same phenomenon, and it would seem that the extra vigor in these triploids, which are highly sterile and probably always autotriploid, having three equal sets of chromosomes), accounts for their widespread occurrence under cultivation. The autotriploids in apples and pears have probably arisen recently and are not completely sterile. Even so, they are less fertile and are maintained because of the predominating asexual propagation of these fruit trees; attempts to breed from the triploids are disastrous, since very poor progenies with unbalanced chromosome numbers result from them. Evidently all the triploid varieties have arisen from the union of haploid and diploid gametes.

In the other fruit trees listed in Table 1.1, polyploids seem to be as common as diploids; however, in the legumes the clear preponderance of diploids is probably owing to the very strong genetic boundaries between species, which prevent hybridization and hence polyploidy. Another interesting phenomenon found in cultivated plants is the frequent occurrence of tetraploids, as in species of cassava, peanut, coffee, and tobacco. Although close diploid relatives of cassava (Manihot) are not yet known, the other plants all possess wild diploid relatives, though present evidence suggests that they were actually brought into cultivation at the tetraploid level.

Most of the polyploid crop species are allopolyploids, that is, polyploids of hybrid origin with clearly marked bivalent pairing. In many cases, as in wheat, plums, cherries, tobacco, and cotton, the original diploid prototypes are well known, though there still are certain areas of doubt (as for instance in the hexaploid oats and the B-genome donor in wheats). Bivalent pairing in wheat polyploids was shown by Riley and Chapman (1958) to be under genetic control, the factor or factors being located in the long arm of chromosome 5B. In the absence of this arm, homoeologous chromosomes pair, thus giving wheat the appearance of an autopolyploid.

In potatoes, on the other hand, all the cultivated polyploids behave to some extent as autopolyploids, even though from experimental evidence we know them to be the results of species hybridization (see Hawkes, 1962; Cribb, 1972). Thus, Swaminathan (1970) and Stebbins (1950) would classify Solanum tuberosum, the common tetraploid potato, as a segmental allopolyploid, that is, an allopolyploid in which some chromosomes or segments in each four "homologous" chromosomes are similar and others are not. However, pairing in this and in the triploids and pentaploids is very irregular. Clearly, marked differentiation of genomes has not occurred in potatoes, with the exception of certain wild Mexican species. Hence the formation of multivalents cannot be taken as evidence of true autopolyploidy.

As far as crop species are concerned, therefore, genetic diversity can accumulate in diploid species just as well as in polyploid species, and, apparently, polyploidy is no more frequent in cultivated plants than it is in wild ones.

Species Concepts

It is interesting to note, as Harlan and others (1973) have pointed out for cereals, that the evolution of domesticates does not always result in the formation of new species, providing that the definition of *species* is a biological one rather than one based on morphology alone. Thus *Triticum bocoticum* (wild diploid wheat) and *T. monococcum* (cultivated diploid wheat) would be considered the same biological species, because they are capable of interbreeding, even though systematists have given the wild progenitor a species name that differs from that of its cultivated descendants. On the other hand, Harlan and others would agree that the hexaploid bread wheats (*T. aestivum*) are distinct from the wild ancestral forms, both diploid and tetraploid. In potatoes, the diploids, and the tetraploids, need to be considered different species because of distinct modes of origin. The tetraploids have originated by a process similar to the one that *T. aestivum* underwent — namely, hybridization, which occurred after the domestication of the species of lesser ploidy.

On the whole, then, these arguments hinge very much on accepted definitions of species. If the biological definition of species is used (see Baker, 1970), one can conclude that most cultigens belong to the same species as their wild progenitors of the same ploidy level, but belong to the different species if they are allopolyploids or segmental allopolyploids. In many instances, however, the wild forms are given varietal or subspecific ranking, or are for convenience classed as separate species.

Disruptive Selection

When within a crop-weed complex there is hybridization between the crop and its wild progenitors or closely related weeds, and the two entities are considered to belong to the same biological species, then the same two types can be recovered in the F_2, or second generation of offspring (see Harlan et al., 1973). The phenomenon of disruptive selection, which selects for two distint adaptive peaks at the same time, has been discussed by Doggett (1965) in the *Sorghum* crop-weed complex, where *S. bicolor* (the crop) and *S. arundinaceum* (the weed) are continually selected from their hybrids by artificial selection for the high-yielding, nonshattering cultivated plants on the one hand and by natural selection of shattering wild-type plants on the other. Many other plants seem to have this kind of relationship, though few have been analyzed in so much detail as *Sorghum*. Such processes of disruptive selection allow crop and weed to maintain their respective adaptive complexes in a satisfactorily integrated state despite their occasional hybridization. The gene pool is maintained as if it were contained in two reservoirs having a filter between them that is usually closed but occasionally opened. Breeders may be able to use this mechanism to determine where new genetic characters can be introduced into the gene pools of cultivated plants so that there are few difficulties and no genetic barriers.

To sum up this chapter, it can be seen that very similar selective processes have been taking place in many different plant species after they have been taken into cultivation. Our ancestors, unconsciously or automatically, selected certain features of plants that made them easier to deal with, such as reduced protective mechanisms, greater ease of collection or harvesting, greater uniformity of germination, and several other characters.

Domestication also brought about greater diversity of plant form and environmental adaptation as our ancestors took plants with them on their wanderings or exchanged them with other tribes. As a consequence, evolution under domestication has been rapid, thus generating the great diversity within crop plants which we see today.

2

The Origins of Agriculture

How did agriculture begin? Was it invented, or did it just happen? Did our ancestors of 10,000 years ago start to "experiment" with plants to see whether they could cultivate them? Did someone with a stroke of inspiration decide how much simpler and more restful it would be to sow wheat, barley or millet around the back door rather than have to continue the wearying food-gathering journeys year after year to keep the family barely alive? These are questions that many have asked, with the unspoken assumption that early men and women were conscious experimenters like ourselves and that they knew, as we do 10,000 years later, that they could get a better living out of those poor grasses and legumes that they had been collecting if they could think of the right way to go about it.

Unfortunately, these speculations are now considered to be far from the truth, although, because no written records exist of how agriculture came about, we must rely on circumstantial evidence and draw conclusions chiefly from the plants themselves. A model based on the evidence from our common domesticated plants, their related wild ancestors, and archaeological findings about early human beings themselves, as shown by their tools and other artifacts, will be useful in investigating just how agriculture probably began.

I have already discussed how archaeological evidence indicates that agriculture had several independent origins at more or less the same point in time. De Candolle (1882) and Vavilov (1926) pointed out that the domestication of most of our crop plants seems to have taken place in several distinct and fairly well-defined areas of the world, mainly within the tropics and subtropics, and generally, though not always, in mountainous regions.

In addition, it is clear that our major domesticated plants have originated from a rather restricted number of plant families, chief among them being Gramineae and Leguminosae, followed by the Cruciferae, Rosaceae, Umbelliferae, Solanaceae, and Labiatae, with the Chenopodiaceae, Araceae, Cucurbitaceae, and Compositae not far behind. Some 20 or 30 families (Vitaceae, Musaceae, Rubiaceae, and so forth) had at least one very successful genus or species, while others have given rise to no important crops at all. No clear explanation has been put forward to account for this situation. It is true that certain families such as Gramineae, Solanaceae, Cruciferae, and Leguminosae are particularly rich in ecological weeds. Others, such as the Araceae, are well adapted to withstand long periods of drought and hence have developed large underground food storage organs. Others again, such as the Rosaceae, have developed particularly fine-flavored, succulent fruits intended for seed dispersal by birds. Yet many families that seem to be appropriate for domestication have offered hardly any plants of interest. This subject clearly needs further thought and investigation.

I have already mentioned that our preagricultural ancestors undoubtedly gathered all kinds of plants for food and other purposes wherever they went and from all over the world. In fact, the gathering or collecting instinct has become so ingrained in humans that we still find such activities supremely satisfying, whether we are gathering wild berries or, in a sublimated form, collecting stamps, coins, antique furniture, or matchboxes. Nevertheless, although many plants have undoubtedly been gathered at one time or another, only an infinitesimal proportion has ever been cultivated.

The Ecological Basis of Agriculture

Why, then, were certain plants cultivated and finally domesticated? If we look at the problem from an ecological point of view, we find that, as I have discussed in Chapter 1, the ancestral forms of crop plants, the "wild prototypes," as they are called, are colonizing species – ecological weeds – and that the crops themselves are also weeds in the ecological sense: they are unable to withstand competition from climax vegetation and respond favorably only to "open" habitats where such competition is at a minimum.

Of course the weedy "ancestors" of cultivated plants that still exist today are not quite so simple as they seem. We cannot consider a "wild prototype" to be the direct ancestor of a crop, since both have been evolving in parallel ever since the two first diverged some 10,000 years ago. Furthermore, there is evidence that the so-called wild prototypes hybridize from time to time with the crop, and each "captures" genes by introgression or limited gene flow with the other. But all in all, we can generally find instances of a crop plant's putative ancestor growing both as a wild species and as a cultivation weed. A good illustration of this point is teosinte, *Zea* (*Euchlaena*) *mexicana*, which not only grows in west-central Mexico as part of the wild vegetation there (in primary habitats undisturbed by man), but also occurs as a weed of maize fields, where, morphologically, it strongly gives the impression of having obtained maize genes by introgression, that is, through partially sterile hybrids (Garrison Wilkes, 1967).

There is thus abundant evidence to show that crops and their wild prototypes possess the character of weediness in common and that many of the derivatives of these wild prototypes can be found in cultivated fields as weeds that grow along with the crops themselves, existing in so-called crop-weed complexes. The plants making up such crop-weed complexes, however, must be clearly distinguished from those ancestral forms that occur in *primary* habitats, of which teosinte provides an example and which is also evident in ancestors of wheat and barley in the Middle East (Zohary, 1969). There, *Hordeum spontaneum*, *Triticum boeoticum*, and *T. dicoccoides* are said to be important herbaceous constituents of the "sub-Mediterranean" belt of oak park–forest vegetation. Such inhabitants of primary habitats as the maize, wheat, and barley ancestors do exhibit weediness, but they have not become weeds in those places because they grow far from human habitation and cultivated fields.

If, therefore, the growth and habitat requirements of the cultivated plants and their present-day closely related wild prototypes are similar, we can reasonably assume that the characteristic of weediness was a strong feature of the original forms from which cultivated plants were derived. Before the advent of man, they must have lived a precarious existence on river banks, sand bars, and game trails, and in areas where landslides occurred or animals wandered or bedded down. It is likely that they were chiefly adapted to regions where poor, thin soil dried out quickly at the end of the rainy season and so prevented the establishment of trees, bushes, and perennial grasses with which our crop ancestors were unable to compete. Harlan and de Wet (1965) argue that since the word *weed* is defined with reference to human habitats, weeds per se could not have existed before human beings. However, there is no reason to believe that a weed defined with reference to the *ecological* habitat could not have existed before man. Weeds could have been growing in the same open areas that people extended so spectacularly through their activities, which enabled these plants, once nature's misfits, to expand their range with great success into the man-made environments.

The Rubbish-Heap Hypothesis

One well-known hypothesis for the origin of agriculture was put forward by Engelbrecht (1916 — see also the translation and commentary by Zeven, 1973). He considered that early humans had gathered nutritious roots and seeds and discarded some of them around their dwellings. Such plants also actively colonized these bare areas, which were enriched by discarded rubbish — the kitchen middens of archaeological terminology. Thus, Engelbrecht concluded that agriculture was not planned by human beings, but that the mere propinquity of such "habitation weeds," as Darlington (1956) later called them, led to its inevitable development.

Both Sauer (1952) and Anderson (1952) seem to adhere to this view, though they make no reference to Engelbrecht's work. They put forward a "rubbish heap," or "dump heap," hypothesis that is the same as Engelbrecht's. It assumes that plants with weedy tendencies colonized kitchen middens and rubbish heaps because these were open habitats to which the plants were already preadapted. People then gathered the seeds or the edible roots, as the case may have been, and gradually brought them into cultivation. Thus, these habitation weeds sought man out as much as he sought them. Such a seemingly magical phenomenon may have given rise to the myths of many agricultural peoples that their crop plants were gifts of the gods. Not only did they appear miraculously on the rubbish heaps around dwellings, but the yields were probably extremely good because of the richness of the soil there, in contrast with the poor soil and consequent poor growth of these plants in their natural habitats.

The rubbish-heap, or habitation-weed, hypothesis for the origin of agriculture seems to fit the facts remarkably well. It assumes no special mental leap on the part of early man, but describes a natural process based on man's known food-gathering activities on the one hand and the ecological requirements of a particular group of plants on the other. Unfortunately, the hypothesis is not perfect. It does not account for the fact that, of all the thousands of weed species that may have colonized the bare ground near human dwellings, only a very few were eventually domesticated. Clearly, some weeds, such as *Atropa belladonna* and *Hyposcyamus niger*, proved poisonous, but even if we discount those, the problem remains. The seeds of many weed species were certainly gathered and eaten, as the stomach contents of the Danish bog-burial people, for instance, show (Glob, 1969), but that did not automatically qualify those plants for cultivation. The hypothesis also does not explain why agriculture began only about 10,000 years ago — certainly a very small fraction of man's existence on this planet.

The Origins of Seed Agriculture

Let us look a little more closely at the origins of seed agriculture. Archaeobotanical evidence for the place of origins of cereals, in both the Old and New Worlds, points to the mountainous regions of the warm temperate to tropical zones with areas having very well marked wet and dry seasons as the regions where agriculture first arose (Braidwood, 1960; Flannery, 1973; Zohary, 1973). Irrigated river valley agriculture probably came much later.

Since we know that plants with weedy tendencies cannot survive competition in a climax forest or in a thick grassland sward, it is reasonable to suppose that they would have been able to grow chiefly only in the poor thin soil of rocky ledges or in poor sandy or gravelly soil that became dessicated in summer droughts. During the rainy season, on the other hand, they might grow there in such quantities as to constitute a kind of ephemeral climax vegetation, influenced by the poor soil and complete drought during the summer months. Such conditions are described by Zohary (1969, p. 57) for Israel, where the wild cereals "shed their fruits and turn into barren dry stalks within one or two weeks." Plants growing in short rainy seasons separated by long droughts must germinate and grow quickly when the rains come, so that their seeds mature before the ground dries out in the summer. Thereafter, they need to survive the drought until the rains begin again and hence they are subjected to strong selection pressure to develop large seeds that can provide sufficient stores of food for quick and sturdy growth when the dry season is over. One could thus say that these plants must have been preadapted for agriculture; no doubt they were of particular interest to man because of their large food reserves. The two attributes of weediness and large food reserves seem to me to provide the key to the domestication of southwest Asian and perhaps also the Meso-American grain crops (Hawkes, 1969). The millets on which Chinese agriculture was originally based have smaller seeds, but perhaps they were the only reasonable source of starch in that region, before the wheats and barleys had been introduced. *Phaseolus* beans, and such ancient New World domesticates as the minor grain crops *Amaranthus* and *Chenopodium*, were also relatively large-seeded and seem to furnish other evidence for this hypothesis. How can we postulate the sequence of events in the development of seed agriculture? Three stages seem to form the continuous process.

1. *Colonization and gathering.* In this first stage the preadapted wild plants with weedy tendencies and large reserves of food began to colonize the open ground or kitchen middens around man's dwellings and were gathered there, as well as from their natural habitats. Also, people probably accidentally dropped seeds from material collected from the natural habitats on the same ground, and thus reinforced the process.

2. *Harvesting.* Gathering is really only another word for harvesting, except the harvesting implies a more orderly process based on a deeper knowledge of the plant. So at this stage of "agriculture," the grains or seeds were probably regularly harvested from the plots around the dwellings; perhaps these plots were fenced in to protect

them from domesticated cattle and wild herbivores. Perhaps, too, people were already selecting mutants for increased yield and palatability, and the plants might have evolved a series of better-adapted ecotypes that were able to take advantage of the richer soil conditions.

I must emphasize that in stages 1 and 2, the wild plant's natural distribution methods (the brittle rachis of a cereal, for instance) were probably still in evidence, and people were not retaining seeds for the next year's sowing. Both stages 1 and 2 developed from the activities of earlier gathering cultures. Although we speak of "man" as undertaking these activities, it is more than likely that women were mainly responsible for the beginnings of crop agriculture; men may have been more involved with hunting and herding.

3. *Sowing*. Because sowing involves an active and careful retention of seeds, placement of them in the soil at the right time, and careful guarding of them at all stages until the time of harvest, this stage must have come very late, when people really began to know their plants, and it thus marks the end of the preagricultural phase. Before this stage, too, mutants having a nonbrittle rachis might have been gathered for consumption but would not be perpetuated, because only the grains from plants with a brittle rachis would fall to the ground and thus become the next crop. At the gathering and harvesting stages, therefore, mutants having the nonbrittle character must have been selected *against*, unconsciously of course. Once the sowing phase began, however, selection pressure changed to *favor* plants with the nonbrittle rachis, because those were the plants that had a better chance of being gathered and hence of forming the store of seeds for the following year's sowing. Only at this third sowing stage, therefore, could the crop be considered truly domesticated, and agriculture to have begun.

It is tempting to ask ourselves how the vital and important transition between stages 2 and 3 came about, though only a tentative answer can be provided at present. We have taken as axiomatic that during the colonization-and-gathering and the harvesting stages, the wild plant grew in the areas near settlements and was continually colonizing kitchen middens and gardens. Let us suppose that this additional source of food led to a considerable increase of population. To have enough food, families would begin to move away from the original area, eventually reaching regions where the wild progenitors no longer grew. Those families could continue to harvest the food plants in the new regions only if they had taken some seeds along with them. Thus not all the harvest could be eaten; some of it was saved for throwing down around the new human colonies – as they had, in effect, seen the plants do. As populations continued to spread, so this new tradition of keeping and sowing seed – a tradition born of necessity – may have become established.

The Origins of Root and Tuber Agriculture

Root and tuber agriculture, or vegeculture, as it is often called, has not received as much attention as seed agriculture, because it has developed mostly in the tropics. Sauer (1952) regarded it as the fundamental process in the beginnings of agriculture, followed only later by seed agriculture. He thought this mainly because early humans might have found the principle upon which root agriculture rests simple: a root is harvested from the soil and planted back into the same place, while a seed is obtained from the top of the plant, a place different from where it is planted. Unfortunately, the archaeological facts do not fit this elegant hypothesis, since in many regions where seed agriculture predominates, there are no root or tuber plants suitable for food; in the tropics, where roots and tubers are so abundantly grown, there may have been no suitable grain crops.

Thus seed agriculture seems to have developed in the mountainous zones of the warm temperate regions of the Old World and in the northern tropical belt of the New World (Sauer, 1952), places where suitable seed plants were available and where ecological conditions were suitable. On the other hand, root and tuber agriculture seems to have developed in the tropical lowlands with a well-marked dry period. However, there are many regions where both exist side by side, though Harris (1969) believes that this is a secondary trend, in which seed agriculture is gradually replacing vegeculture. He also points to the highly generalized ecosystems with polycultures, that is to say, of many plant species growing together, in the vegeculture type of agriculture, while seed agriculture tends to be monocultural (one plant species in a field). Nevertheless, in the tropics, and even in temperate zones at an early stage, agriculture was probably always very mixed.

It has been suggested by Sauer (1952) and by Harris (1969) that vegeculture originated on the edges of dry forest zones, or in the ecotones (transition zones) between major ecosystems such as forest and savannah. Plants with food supplies stored in their roots, tubers, and rhizomes *must* have evolved in areas with a well-marked dry season (perhaps from three to seven dry months), because otherwise there would have been no selection pressure to build up such reserves, which man has since used to great advantage.

The actual vegetation zones where various vegecultural crops developed were probably not identical. Yams and sweet potatoes may have evolved in summer-green forest, since they need the trees and bushes of such areas to climb on. On the other hand, crops with short stems, such as taro (*Colocasia*), cassava (*Manihot*), and others, probably evolved in summer-green scrub or semidesert areas. There are also cool-mountain tuber crops in the New World tropics — potatoes, oca (*Oxalis tuberosa*), ulluco (*Ullucus tuberosus*), and several others — that must have originated in seasonally dry upland valleys and intermont basins, very doubtfully in woodland. Thus, knowledge of the ecological requirements of the crops acts as a pointer to the likely phytogeographical regions where they were originally domesticated.

Some doubt exists as to whether vegeculture is as old as seed agriculture. The problem is that the climatic conditions of areas where vegeculture probably began are generally not very good for long-term storage, though there is archaeological evidence at least for the origins of potatoes in Peru some 8,000 years before the present (B.P.) (Martins, 1976), where storage conditions on the coast and in the drier mountain valleys are very good. Nevertheless, the three stages of the origins of seed agriculture are essentially the same as those of vegeculture.

1. *Colonization and gathering.* Plants probably first became established on the rubbish heaps or kitchen middens around the habitations, either because pieces of the roots or tubers gathered from afar were discarded there, or because seeds deposited naturally there had good conditions for growth.

2. *Harvesting.* Harvesting developed naturally from stage 1, as it did for seed agriculture. A selection for short stolons or rhizomes might begin to take place at this stage.

3. *Planting.* Planting most likely developed under "slash / burn,"

or swidden agriculture, since roots and tubers had to be provided for each forest clearing in which the crops were to be grown. At this stage, plants having short stolons and rhizomes were at a strong selective advantage, because the roots or tubers developing on long ones tended to be lost, or at any rate were not harvested so frequently and hence were not taken so often to the new plots when families moved on.

My researches with the potato show a number of modern examples where stage 2 harvesting is continuous but where planting is absent or only intermittent. In the slash / burn method of agriculture in parts of Guatemala and Colombia, potatoes are harvested for three or four years after the initial sowing, and this is discontinued only when the soil becomes too depleted in nutrients to bear a further crop. Of even more interest is that in parts of the western Andes of Venezuela, the harvesting of potatoes from kitchen gardens is continuous, since some tubers are always left in the soil for further growth during the following year. The proximity of the garden to the house means that the soil is continually being enriched from nutrients in the domestic rubbish thrown onto it, a situation that therefore seems to be a relic of the second, or harvesting, phase in the evolution of agriculture.

The Time Scale of Agricultural Origins

Why did agriculture develop so late in our cultural history? We know that the plants were available millions of years before the beginnings of agriculture, and we are therefore forced to turn to nonbotanical evidence to try to solve the problem.

Sauer (1952) and others have stressed that a settled mode of existence is an essential prerequisite for agriculture. This seems logical, since man needs to develop a relationship with his plants that can be permanent only if he continually lives in the same place. However, others, such as MacNeish (1972), have suggested that if communities regularly moved from lower regions in winter to higher ones in summer (transhumance), the beginnings of farming could still have taken place. People would return to their plots or "bare-soil areas" at certain times of the year to harvest the cereals and other crops, which in their absence had, as it were, grown like a gift from the gods. Such practices are still common among Indian tribes in the Chocó region of Colombia. Very primitive varieties of maize are sown by scattering grain at random in a freshly made swidden plot. At the time of crop maturity, the Indians return to harvest the yield.

Sauer postulated that what he called "well-situated, progressive fishing folk living in a mild climate along fresh waters" were those most likely to be in a position to initiate farming. He decided on fresh, rather than salt waters, pointing out that "seaside vegetation has contributed little and late to the making of crop plants." Even so, a number of our crops, such as spinach, beet, amaranths, and celery, do react favorably to the presence of salt. It is considered, however, that these plants either came into cultivation late or were derived from races adapted to the saline soils of the margins of the great Middle-Eastern salt deserts rather than to maritime soils. Sauer therefore concluded that the year-round supply of "harvestable" animals such as snails, fresh water mussels, small fish, and water birds meant that communities could settle in one place permanently and thus meet the prerequisites for farming. This hypothesis seems reasonable, and few would now seriously disagree with it.

Many researchers have proposed climatic changes as the reasons for the adoption of agriculture at a particular point in time, pointing to the approximate synchroneity of agriculture in the Near East, the Far East, and Meso-America. However, Braidwood (1960) does not believe that the climatic changes taking place after the retreat of the glaciers about 10,000 years ago could have accounted entirely for the beginnings of agriculture, since similar changes had taken place on other occasions in the last 75,000 years. Recent studies have indicated also that there was no spectacular climatic change at that time, though others disagree with this idea. Braidwood concludes that the answer must lie in the ever-increasing cultural development and specialization of human communities, which had arrived at the correct stage of tool making and of social organization only some 10,000 years ago.

Flannery (1973) feels that caution should be exercised in attributing the origin of agriculture to a single cause. He agrees that it took place toward the end of a steadily ameliorating climatic period, that the population of the area was significantly higher than at any time previously, and that the inhabitants were living in settled communities, gathering various "harvestable" invertebrates and wild cereal grasses. He feels, however, and I am inclined to agree with him, that the increase in the number of sedentary communities and the changes in their sociopolitical organization were the key features here.

Very interesting information has been provided by van Zeist (1970) and Casparie (van Zeist and Casparie, 1968). They have found evidence of communities at Tell Mureybit in northern Syria that gathered wild einkorn wheat (*Triticum boeoticum*) and wild barley (*Hordeum spontaneum*) in large quantities. Radiocarbon dating suggests an age for the grain of between 9,500 and 10,400 years before the present. Other wild species, particularly lentils and vetches, were also found in the samples. The Tell Mureybit peoples, who lived on the banks of the upper Euphrates and probably ate animal food of the type mentioned, had no domesticated animals and were clearly at a food-gathering cultural stage. Since wild einkorn wheat is not now found on the plains of northern Syria, van Zeist suggested that the people traveled some 100 kilometers north to Turkey, where it now grows, to gather their food supplies. However, it seems to me more likely that a slight shift of climate, or circumstances in which grazing pressure was not so intense as it is nowadays, would have provided conditions for the cereals to grow as wild species in the general region of Tell Mureybit itself. Van Zeist, however, is not willing to suppose, from the evidence available, that the climate was significantly different from that of the present. Very relevant information on grazing pressures in Israel is provided by Zohary (1969, p. 56), who shows that when grazing pressure is relaxed, the wild grasses, including of course the wild cereals, reestablish their dominance within a few years, while under heavy grazing, their place is often taken by less-palatable herbs. I am therefore inclined to suspect that the inhabitants of Tell Mureybit may even have been at the phase of incipient agriculture, in stages 1 and 2 of colonization and harvesting, which I postulated earlier. Because at those stages the mutations for a nonbrittle rachis would not yet have been selected for, one would expect archaeological remains to be of the "wild-type," which indeed they are. Furthermore, the plants could indeed have flourished in the absence of grazing pressures, since the Tell Mureybit people had not yet domesticated any cattle.

I have discussed at length the beginnings of agriculture in the

Near East, because perhaps more research has been done on that area than on any other. However, much useful information now exists on early Chinese agriculture (see Chang, 1970; Ping-Ti Ho, 1969, 1976). It seems clear that the earliest Neolithic agricultural sites are to be found in northern China on the loess soil terraces along various tributaries of the Yellow River. The plant remains are of *Setaria italica* and *Panicum miliaceum* (*shu* and *chi*, respectively), and unequivocal evidence exists for their cultivation by at least Yangshao times, some 7,000 years ago. The evidence for rice cultivation in the same area suggests it began about 5,000 years ago at the earliest. We do not yet know the details of settlement and cultivation practices, and we lack evidence such as that provided by van Zeist of any preagricultural gathering economy, but these will probably be forthcoming when more information is released from mainland China.

Although Sauer (1952) contended that the earliest beginnings of agriculture were to be found in Southeast Asia (see Fig. 2.1), particularly because of its fishing and farming culture and the many vegecultural crops there, which he considered a priori to have been brought into cultivation earlier than seed crops, there are very little archaeological data to support this. The earliest plant remains from this region come from Spirit Cave in northwest Thailand (Gorman, 1969) and have been radiocarbon-dated back to 9180±360 B.P. However, Gorman does not postulate that these were cultivated, and Flannery (1973) urges caution in relying on the interpretations of the data by others who have made exaggerated claims for the antiquity of horticulture in this area. Gorman himself made no such claims, and "his presentation of the Spirit Cave data was cautious and reasonable" (Flannery, 1973). No major crop plant was identified, and one feels on examining the list of plant seeds and fruits discovered that they might well be evidence of a food-gathering culture and no more.

Perhaps the biggest enigma of all is Africa. Egypt seems to have been moving toward agriculture in very early times, but this gradual process was overtaken by the introduction of wheats and barleys from the Near East (Harlan, 1975c). There seem to be centers of plant diversity in Ethiopia and in west tropical Africa, but the evidence is conflicting as to whether agriculture began independently in those two regions: Anderson (1960), Portères (1962), and others

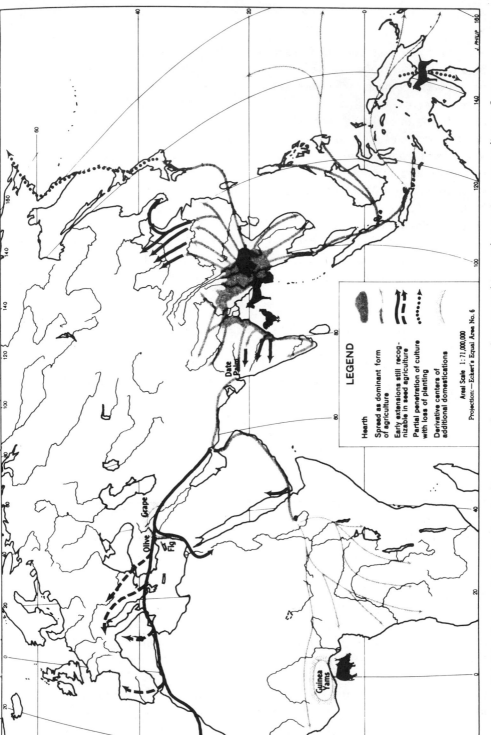

Fig 2.1 Presumed origins of agriculture in Southeast Asia and its spread into other regions, according to Sauer. (From Sauer, 1969; reprinted with the permission of the American Geographical Society.)

LEGEND

Hearth

Spread as dominant form of agriculture

Early extensions still recognizable in seed agriculture

Partial penetration of culture with loss of planting

Derivative centers of additional domestications

Areal Scale 1:71,000,000
Projection:—Eckert's Equal Area No. 6

Date Palm

Olive

Grape

Fig

Guinea Yams

J. PHILIP

were inclined to think that it did; Harlan (1971) was very doubtful. An almost complete lack of early achaeological data renders this problem impossible to solve for the moment. The matter is discussed in detail also by Harris (1967) and Harlan (1975c).

Evidence for early agriculture in Meso-America, on the other hand, is much more abundant and is clearly indicative of ancient agricultural horizons, owing in no small measure to MacNeish and his co-workers (MacNeish, 1964, 1965; Mangelsdorf, MacNeish, and Willey, 1970). There is evidence that by about 7,000 B.P. cultivation of *Phaseolus* beans, cucurbits (squashes), amaranths, chili peppers, and maize had begun (Bray, 1977). (See Fig. 2.2.) It is difficult to be certain that all the early plant remains were already cultivated, but the evidence indicates very clearly that maize and *Phaseolus vulgaris* were being grown by 7,000 B.P., and that many other cultigens appeared later, certainly by 5,000 B.P. The early remains of maize at Tehuacán are claimed by Mangelsdorf, MacNeish, and Galinat (1967) to be wild, but most other palaeoethnobotanists would maintain that they were already cultivated, because the grains are arranged in a cob of several rows, while the truly wild related grasses such as *Zea mexicana* and *Tripsacum* possess single-rowed, easily shattering spikes. Most researchers familiar with the subject now believe the wild ancestor of maize to be the wild grass teosinte (*Zea mexicana*); although it does not seem particularly appetizing, it has some of the properties of a popcorn, and it also possesses weedy tendencies, as I have already stated. Squashes, peppers, and amaranths are also weedy in nature and could easily have colonized bare patches of ground near settlements. An interesting "human ecology" study has been carried out by Flannery (1973) and his colleagues in an attempt to quantify yields for the different prototypes of the plants brought into cultivation some 7,000 years ago. This provides much valuable information on possible early agricultural patterns.

Finally, some mention should be made of agricultural origins in the Andes of South America, since it has been postulated that agriculture originated independently in that region also. There the problem is one of the scarcity of preserved plant remains in the highland zone and humid eastern slopes, though the extremely rich remains in the desert of the western coast amply compensate for it. A list of plants grown on the Peruvian coast at Ancón-Chillón is given by Bray (1976). (See Fig. 2.3.)

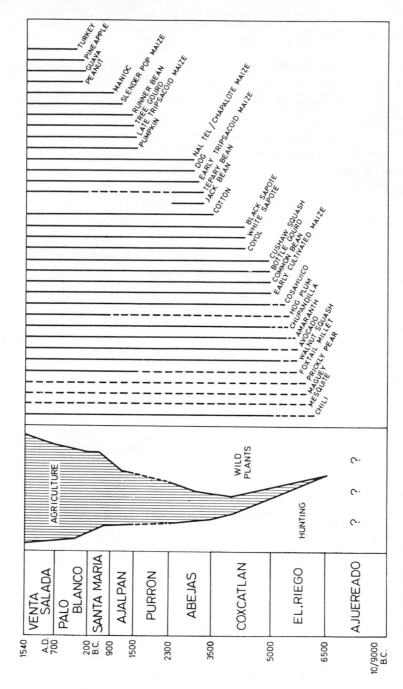

Fig 2.2 Agricultural evolution and plant domestication in the Tehuacán Valley, Mexico. Bottle gourd, perhaps cultivated, is now reported for the period 8000–6000 B.C. The sieva bean (*Ph. lunatus*) was introduced during the Venta Salada phase, and the pumpkin may have been cultivated by the Abejas period. (Bray, 1976.)

Fig. 2.3 Settlement pattern, subsistence and population in the Ancón-Chillón region of the central Peruvian coast. Population figures are from Patterson (1971b); Cohen (1973) prefers a higher estimate. The common bean, avocado, ciruela, manioc, and campomanesia were introduced soon after 900 B.C.; llama and guinea pig were domesticated from 200 B.C.; *Cucurbita maxima* first appears after A.D. 1000; quinoa, cherimoya, and (?) oca were not introduced until the Inca period. All supplementary data are abstracted from Cohen (1973). (Bray, 1976.)

Date	CULTURAL PERIOD	SUBSISTENCE & SETTLEMENT	Estimated population
1200 B.C.	INITIAL CERAMIC PERIOD	MAIN SITES LARGE & INLAND. SMALL-SCALE IRRIGATION UPSTREAM. SPECIALIZED FARMING & FISHING SITES	Rapid growth
1750			1500
	GAVIOTA	VERY LARGE COASTAL SITES. SETTLEMENT HIERARCHY, SITES WITH SPECIALIZED COASTAL & INLAND FARMING ACTIVITIES	1000–1500
1850	CONCHAS	LARGE PERMANENT COASTAL VILLAGES, LITTORAL COLLECTION & FLOODWATER FARMING. SMALL-SCALE LOCAL EXCHANGES	500
2275	PLAYA HERMOSA	SMALL PERMANENT COASTAL VILLAGES. MAINLY LITTORAL COLLECTION & FLOODWATER FARMING	300
2500	ENCANTO	INLAND SEASONAL CAMPS. MARINE & INLAND RESOURCES, LITTLE FLOODWATER AGRICULTURE	100–200
3800			50–100
4200	CORBINA	SMALL SEASONAL INLAND CAMPS.	50
	CANARIO	EXPLOITATION OF COAST & VALLEY FLOOR	50–100
5000 B.C.			

CULTIVATED PLANTS (first appearance, earliest to latest): BOTTLE GOURD, *C. moschata*, *C. ficus*, SQUASHES, COTTON, CHILI, GUAVA, JACK BEAN, ACHIRA, LIMA BEAN, PEANUT, LUCUMA, ACHUPALLA, PACAY, MAIZE, SWEET POTATO

Theories of "verticality" postulate that communities worked vertical strips of land that extended from the coast to altitudes of several thousand meters, and such ideas are now becoming very popular (Murra, 1972). These indicate that there must have been much interchange of food resources between coast and mountains, and therefore, remains found along the coast might also give a good idea of what was grown in the mountains. Moseley (1972) postulates from his work in the Ancón region of central Peru that there was an intermediate stage between hunting and gathering on the one hand and farming on the other. This stage was, according to him, a marine subsistence economy where fishing and shellfish gathering perdominated and plants were used only in limited ways. These events, he states, took place between 5,000 and 3,000 B.P. Martins (1976), however, having analyzed Moseley's plant remains, found substantial evidence for clearly cultivated plants, some of which, such as cassava and sweet potato, had probably been grown at or near Ancón, and others of which, such as potatoes, oca (*Oxalis tuberosa*), and ulluco (*Ullucus tuberosus*), would have been grown at higher altitudes in the mountains (at 3,000–4,000 meters perhaps), possibly as part of the vertical crop exchange or communal agricultural systems referred to by Murra (1972). In Engel's Chilca canyon excavations (1970), Martins identified a similar range of food products, with one sample of potatoes, believed to be cultivated, going back to 8,000 B.P.

These studies were all concerned with samples of vegeculture, but one cannot argue from them that seed agriculture was not present in the early stages of farming in the Andes, for two reasons. First, both Mosely and Engel purposely sent tuber material to Martins because she was working in my laboratory and they hoped we would be able to tell whether the material could or could not be identified as potatoes. Other plant materials were no doubt sent elsewhere. Second, there is excellent evidence from the Guitarrero Cave in the Callejón de Huaylas, Ancash, Peru, that *Phaseolus vulgaris* and *P. lunatus* were being cultivated as early as 7,680 ± 280 to 10,000 ± 300 B.P. (Kaplan, Lynch, and Smith, 1973). The evidence for cultivation is unequivocal, both on the basis of seed size and patterning and on the evidence of pod structure. Furthermore, the materials were taken from a dry site of mesic-climatic type, not very different from that of Tehuacán in Mexico and the mountainous regions of the Fertile Crescent in the Near East.

All this information seems to support very strongly the hypothesis that prerequisites for the origins of agriculture were (1) climatic, in the sense that areas with well-marked dry seasons were necessary; (2) ecological, in that the earliest domesticates were ecological weeds – species of plants able, as opportunists and colonizers, to invade bare ground and to take advantage of high levels of nutrients around caves or huts; (3) taxonomic, in that the plants came from a limited range of families, but whether they were grasses, legumes, cucurbits, tuber plants, or some other group, all had weediness in common; and (4) physiological – the seeds, tubers, or roots had large food reserves to tide them over a long dry season and for this reason were of interest to man. Whether specific rainfall or temperature conditions, certain densities of human population, or certain levels of socioeconomic organization were needed is a little more doubtful and these issues still need much study and discussion. Indeed, we would be very rash to say that we have now solved the mysteries of agricultural origins, though undoubtedly much progress has been made.

For the plant breeder and student of plant evolution, several conclusions can be drawn from these studies. The first concerns the weedy nature of crop plants, developed from wild species that were themselves ecological weeds and that were closely related to ones existing today. It is true that for some crops, such as broad beans (*Vicia faba*), no living wild prototype has yet been discovered and perhaps may not now exist. Nevertheless, for nearly all other crops, related weed species or forms are known and seem to have evolved in close contact with the crop in its ancient center of diversity, often introgressing with it. Much variability exists in these weed forms, and this has been useful to breeders in the past and may be of great value now and in the future.

The second conclusion concerns the fact that agriculture began, and other crops were later domesticated, in regions with well-marked wet and dry seasons, neither of which were excessively long (see Harris, 1969, p. 10). Thus, if we wish to explore the world for promising new crops, we might well search in such areas for plants that have evolved ways to survive a long dry season by storing up large food reserves. At the same time we should be searching for the ecological weeds rather than the long-lived woody or shrubby perennials.

Finally, we might pay special attention to those plant families that have been so successful in providing us with food and other materials of economic value. Thus, aroids, yams, and other root and tuber plants in the tropics, as well as tropical grain legumes, should be examined, and researchers should concentrate on those that are collected, but not yet cultivated, by peoples who are still in an early stage of cultural development.

3

The Study of Crop Plant Evolution
and Dispersal

The evolution of crop plants under domestication has given rise to more diversity, and of a more complex nature, than can be seen in any comparable group of wild plants. As Edgar Anderson (1960) so wisely put it, "The origin of a cultivated plant is a process, not an event," and by this he certainly must have meant that the evolution of a plant species did not cease, but on the contrary became more intense and diversified, once it had been domesticated.

Throughout the development of botanical thought, right up to the early nineteenth century, our basic crop plants received very little attention. The medieval and Renaissance herbalists were much more interested in the wild medicinal plants that needed to be identified and gathered to make up their remedies and prescriptions. Some of these plants were grown in herb gardens, but because they were transplanted from the wild, they were botanically more or less identical to wild plants. Crop plants, on the other hand, were of very little interest to the early botanists, who, apart from fitting the plants into their systems of classification and providing descriptions and figures, paid hardly any more attention to them.

So, as late as the beginning of the nineteenth century, the well-known traveler and naturalist Baron von Humboldt was forced to sum up the situation in his *Essai sur las géographie des plantes* (1807), as follows: "The origin, the first home of the plants most useful to man, and which have accompanied him from the remotest epochs, is a secret as impenetrable as the dwelling of all our domestic animals ... We do not know what region produced spontaneously, wheat, barley, oats and rye. The plants which constitute the natural riches of all the inhabitants of the tropics, the banana, the pawpaw, the manoic and maize have never been found in the wild state."

This work no doubt acted as a stimulus to Alphonse de Candolle, a Swiss botanist and phytogeographer who, in his *Géographie botanique raisonnée* (1855) and *Origine des plantes cultivées* (1882), was the first to make a special study of cultivated plants and their history. De Candolle's greatest contribution was to focus attention for the first time on the complex history of cultivated plants, and he laid down a series of precepts or suggestions for their study, pointing out pitfalls in the various methods of investigation. Many of his conclusions are untenable today chiefly owing to advances in genetics, cytology, comparative phytochemistry, and archaeology. Furthermore, he did not examine the taxonomy of the crops and their wild relatives in sufficient detail. However, his *Origines des plantes cultivées*, especially the concluding chapters, was a masterly review of the historical, linguistic, and archaeological data available at that time.

For agriculture to begin, de Candolle thought that the following conditions should be present:

1. A suitable plant should be available.
2. The climate should not be too rigorous.
3. There should be security and a settled mode of living.
4. There should be a pressing need for food, such as insufficient game, a restricted terrain (such as enclosed mountain valleys), or no abundant plant that was there for the picking.

Nowadays we pay much more attention to ecological studies in elucidating the origins of domesticated plants, developing the first and third points much more than the others.

Establishing the Point of Origin of a Crop Plant

How is one to decide the place of origin of a cultivated plant? De Candolle thought that one could tell where a plant was first domesticated by finding out where it grew wild, but it is often difficult to determine whether a plant in a particular area is truly wild or is an escape from cultivation. Information from published Floras, or from travelers and collectors lacking the specialist's knowledge, is often incorrect. Even if correct information is obtained about a wild plant, one must be cautious in making too many assumptions. Sometimes one cannot tell at all where a plant originated, as is the case with *Vicia faba*, the broad bean, because no wild ancestor has yet been found. Nor is location in the wild a good criterion for deciding on the origin of such plants as tomatoes: the various wild species grow in Peru, while other evidence shows that cultivated tomatoes probably originated in Mexico.

In other cases, what were once thought to have been wild ancestral species of a crop plant have later been shown to be quite unrelated to it. For example, we now know that the wild potatoes of Chile, Uruguay, and Mexico, which were at one time thought to have been the prototypes of our domestic potato, are clearly distinct species, having different chromosome numbers and being taxonomically remote from the cultigen.

Sometimes the wild species has become naturalized and is very abundant in a region where it is not indigenous. For example, prickly-pear cactus (*Opuntia ficus-indica*) and agave (*Agave americana*) are common in the Mediterranean but were introduced there comparatively recently from Mexico. Domestication certainly took place in Mexico, not in the Mediterranean basin.

De Candolle pointed out the great value of archaeological evidence for establishing a plant's origin. Although we have no truly fossilized cultivated plants, we have plenty of well-preserved and dried seed, fruit, and pollen remains that enable us to follow the course of evolution in certain crops such as maize and wheat to an extent that has never been done with wild plants. So the provision of a fourth, time dimension provides information on cultivated plants that is frustratingly absent when one studies wild plants. This is another important reason why the study of cultivated plants is so important for our understanding of plant evolution.

Historical evidence is in many cases of little use. The domestication of all our major crop plants took place long before the dawn of written history, so that all we can use are folk legends and myths. Since the ancient historians often copied from each other, one must be careful to look for several *independent* sources of information as corroborative evidence. There are many historical errors that have been perpetuated from early times. For example, the Romans thought that peaches first came from Persia, because that was where they found them: hence the Latin name *Prunus persica*. We now know that peaches were first domesticated in China and had reached Persia by Roman times. The pomegranate is Persian in origin, but by Roman times it had spread to Carthage, hence its name *Punica granatum*.

Linguistic evidence for plant origins can be even more misleading, especially since one can never be absolutely certain of the identity of the plant referred to in ancient languages. Even in recent times the apparently haphazard and erroneous naming of plants is worrying, to say the least. For example, why should the French term for maize have been *blé de Turquie*? This is a New World plant with no possible links to Turkey. Then again, the Jerusalem artichoke (*Helianthus tuberosus*) comes from Canada and the United States, not the Holy Land, as the name implies. Its English name is no more than a corruption of the Italian *gira sol* ("turning to the sun" — sunflower). In France this same plant was called *topinambour*, the name of a tribe of Brazilian Indians who were brought to Paris in the seventeenth century and were presented at court, an event that everyone was talking about. At the same time, the Jerusalem artichoke was offered for sale in the street stalls of Paris, and the name of the exotic tribe was "naturally" applied to the plant.

A similar confusion of names has occurred with the potato, *Solanum tuberosum*, a South American plant. The name *potato* is derived from *batata*, the Caribbean Indian word for what we now call the sweet potato, *Ipomoea batatas*. When this latter plant arrived from Columbus's first voyage, it came with its Arawak Indian name *batata*, which in Spanish became *patata*. When the *Solanum* potato arrived, it was given the same name, *patata*, from which the English word *potato* derives. At least the place of origin of the word *tomato*, derived from the Mexican Aztec word *tomatl*, agrees with the point of origin of the cultivated tomato plant, but this should be considered a lucky coincidence, certainly not an example of a fixed law.

The identity of a plant name in various languages may mean either a relatively recent migration of peoples or the passing of the plant from one group to the next. Names that are cognates indicate rather more ancient usage of the plant in question. Completely dissimilar names *may* mean great aniquity or not. Philologists, as de Candolle has said, do not allow sufficiently for chance and for human stupidity and ingenuity. Clearly, historical and linguistic information must be employed with extreme caution and used only to reinforce botanical, genetic, and archaeological data. De Candolle himself pointed out the need for combining various approaches in this way.

The Contributions of N. I. Vavilov to Crop Plant Origins

N I Vavilov, a Russian botanist (1887-1941), began his studies of crop plants with the very practical purpose of breeding new varieties for the widely differing ecological conditions of the Soviet Union. To do this, he felt it necessary to explore the total genetic diversity of crop plants throughout the world, as well as that of related wild species. He paid very careful attention to farming systems, utilization of the crops, and the ethnobotany of each region he visited. Copious notes and collection data were gathered, together with climatic information, to provide the maximum information possible on each crop and each agricultural region. Even though Vavilov's expeditions were conducted in the 1920s and 1930s, his methods can hardly be bettered today, and they have served as a model to those of us who have come after him. He clearly pioneered the whole subject of the genetic diversity of crop plants.

Before Vavilov's time, plant breeders were content to make crosses and selections based on local varieties, rather than of those from different areas of the world. Vavilov's inspired idea to seek what is now known as a "broad genetic base" for his work on breeding cannot be criticized, even though some of his theories have been the subject of unfavorable comment.

The collections of living specimens, which were brought back and evaluated at the Institute of Plant Industry in Leningrad and in substations in different parts of the Soviet Union, formed the basis for much of the well-known research on breeding that has since been done. For the first time, plant breeders began to look at the total genetic diversity of our ancient crop plants as well as related wild species. Very detailed morphological and cytogenetic studies often helped to clarify the taxonomy of a species very considerably. Vavilov showed that cultivated species, during the course of their dispersion from their areas of origin, had become differentiated into distinct morphological, ecological, and geographical groups. He thus established for cultivated plants "the concept of a Linnaean species as definite, discrete, dynamic system differentiated into geographical and ecological types and comprising sometimes an enormous number of varieties" (Vavilov, 1940).

Although the practical breeder was not very concerned with definitions of Linnaean species, many breeders *were* interested in Vavilov's living materials as bricks with which to build new varieties. Students of the genetics and ecology of cultivated plants then, as now, were interested particularly in Vavilov's agroecological groups, which classified the multiplicity of crop plant variants on an ecogeographical basis, thus enabling breeders to choose materials with a greater likelihood of success in a breeding program (Vavilov, 1957).

Centers of Origin and Diversity

As a result of the multidisciplinary studies carried out on the materials brought back by the Russian expeditions, Vavilov found that there were certain areas of the world where crop plant diversity was extremely intense and others where it was rather slight. The areas, or centers of greatest diversity were believed by Vavilov to represent centers of origin for the crops concerned, and he described and mapped them as such. Centers of diversity of crop after crop were shown to coincide with each other and to possess all sorts of endemic varieties, alleles, and even Linnaean species where plant breeders had not previously had the remotest idea that such genetic richness existed. (Table 3.1).

Vavilov's equation of centers of origin with centers of diversity is to some extent derived from Willis's age-and-area hypothesis (1922), which stated that the greater the distribution area or the greater the number of related species occurring in an area, the older was the genus to which they belonged. Vavilov then postulated that if the mutation rate was constant, and if selective forces remained constant in a species or group, then the longer the plant had existed in a region, the more complex it would become, and the greater would be its area of distribution. Hence, he deduced that the centers of diversity corresponded to centers of ancient origin of the crops concerned. That this is now generally considered an oversimplification should not detract from the value of such a hypothesis to lead others to examine the facts, to work with the plant material, and to try to improve on the original concept.

The amount and quality of genetic variation in crop plants was Vavilov's basis for proposing his centers of origin hypothesis. He began with five centers in 1926, and recombined some and added others from time to time, until he reached eight, with three subcenters (Vavilov, 1935, 1951). (See Fig. 3.1.) Later authors, such as Darlington (1973), have increased the number of centers to 16. Portères (1950, 1962) suggested four independent "cradles" of agriculture for Africa alone. Zhukovsky (1975), Vavilov's colleague, proposed a series of twelve megacenters (Fig. 3.2) that covered almost the whole world, leaving out only Canada, Brazil, southern Argentina, northern Siberia, and such small countries as Norway and Britain. Microcenters of wild-growing species genetically related to the cultivated species are also proposed by Zhukovsky. His systems, I think, point nicely to the differences in distribution between the wild species, which on the whole are very limited in their distribution, and the cultivated species, which have become widespread through the agency of man and have accordingly increased tremendously in their variability. Zhukovsky distinguishes between "primary gene microcenters" — as the the restricted areas where the cultigens first originated — and "secondary gene megacenters," which are the areas into which the cultigens have now spread. Thus, as I see it, he is attempting to meet the criticisms of those who complain that Vavilov's "centers of origin" are not centers at all, but enormously wide areas. The word center is a misnomer in this context, and a phrase such as "total distribution area" might be more accurate.

Harlan (1951) has used the term *microcenter* in a sense different from Zhukovsky's to distinguish very small areas of varietal richness within a Vavilovian center. Such small areas, as Harlan showed for Turkey, contain varietal diversity of several crops, not confined to the plains or the mountains, near civilization or remote from it, nor with primitive or advanced husbandry. Evolution seems to be progressing rapidly in such centers, and Harlan advocates intensive surveys of them (see Figs. 3.3, 3.4, 3.5).

Table 3.1 World centers of diversity of cultivated plants.

1. CHINA

Avena nuda, naked oat (secondary center of origin)
Glycine hispida, soybean
Phaseolus angularis, adzuki bean
Phaseolus vulgaris bean (recessive form; secondary center)
Phyllostachys spp., small bamboos
Brassica juncea, leaf mustard (secondary center of origin)
Prunus armeniaca, apricot
Prunus persica, peach
Citrus sinensis, orange
Sesamum indicum, sesame (endemic group of dwarf varieties; secondary center)
Camellia (Thea) sinensis, China tea

2. INDIA

Oryza sativa, rice
Eleusine coracana, African millet
Cicer arietinum, chickpea
Phaseolus aconitifolius, moth bean
Phaseolus calcaratus, rice bean
Dolichos biflorus, horse gram
Vigna sinensis, asparagus bean
Solanum melongena, eggplant
Raphanus caudatus, rat's tail radish
Colocasia antiquorum, taro yam
Cucumis sativus, cucumber
Gossypium arboreum, tree cotton, 2×
Corchorus olitorius, jute
Piper nigrum, pepper
Indigofera tinctoria, indigo

2.a INDO-MALAYA

Dioscorea spp., yam
Citrus maxima, pomelo
Musa spp., banana
Cocos nucifera, coconut

3. CENTRAL ASIA

Triticum aestivum, bread wheat
Triticum compactum, club wheat
Triticum sphaerococcum, shot wheat
Secale cereale, rye (secondary center)
Pisum sativum, pea
Lens esculenta, lentil
Cicer arietinum, chickpea
Sesamum indicum, sesame (a center of origin)
Linum usitatissimum, flax (a center of origin)
Carthamus tinctorius, safflower (a center of origin)
Daucus carota, carrot (basic center of Asiatic varieties)
Raphanus sativus, radish (a center of origin)
Pyrus communis, pear
Pyrus malus, apple
Juglans regia, walnut

4. THE NEAR EAST

Triticum monococcum, einkorn wheat
Triticum durum, durum wheat
Triticum turgidum, Poulard wheat
Triticum aestivum, bread wheat (endemic awnless group; a center of origin)
Hordeum vulgare cultivated two-rowed barleys (endemic group)
Secale cereale, rye
Avena byzantina, red oat
Cicer arietinum, chick pea (secondary center)
Lens esculenta, lentil (a large endemic group of varieties)
Pisum sativum, pea (a large endemic group; secondary center)
Medicago sativa, blue alfalfa
Sesamum indicum, sesame (a separate geographic group)

Table 3.1 *continued*

Linum usitatissimum, flax (many endemic
varieties)
Cucumis melo, melon
Amygdalus communis, almond
Ficus carica, fig
Punica granatum, pomegranate
Vitis vinifera, grape
Prunus armeniaca, apricot (a center of
origin)
Pistacia vera, pistachio (a center of
origin)

5   THE MEDITERRANEAN

Triticum durum, durum wheat
Avena strigosa, hulled oats
Vicia faba, broad bean
Brassica oleracea, cabbage
Olea europaea, olive
Lactuca sativa, lettuce

6.   ABYSSINIA

Triticum durum, durum wheat (an
amazing wealth of forms)
Triticum turgidum, Poulard wheat (an
exceptional wealth of forms)
Triticum dioccum, Emmer
Hordeum vulgare, barley (an exceptional
diversity of forms)
Cicer arietinum, chickpea (a center of
origin)
Lens esculenta, lentil (a center of origin)
Eragrostis abyssinica, teff
Eleusine coracana, african millet
Pisum sativum, pea (a center of origin)
Linum usitatissimum, flax (a center of
origin)

Sesamum indicum, sesame (basic center)
Ricinus communis, castor bean (a center
of origin)
Coffea arabica, coffee

7.   SOUTHERN MEXICO AND CENTRAL AMERICA

Zea mays, corn
Phaseolus vulgaris, common bean
Capsicum annuum, pepper
Gossypium hirsutum, upland cotton
Agave sisalana, sisal hemp
Cucurbita spp., squash, pumpkin, gourd

8.   SOUTH AMERICA (PERU, ECUADOR, BOLIVIA)

Ipomoea batatas, sweet potato
Solanum tuberosum, potato
Phaseolus lunatus, lima bean
Lycopersicum esculentum, tomato
Gossypium barbadense, sea island cotton
(4×)
Carica papaya, papaya
Nicotiana tabacum, tobacco

8a.   CHILOE

Solanum tuberosum, potato

8b.   BRAZIL AND PARAGUAY

Manihot utilissima, manioc
Arachis hypogaea, peanut
Theobroma cacao, cacao (secondary
center)
Hevea brasiliensis, rubber tree
Ananas comosa, pineapple
Passiflora edulis, purple granadilla

Source: From Zohary, 1970, after Vavilov, 1951.

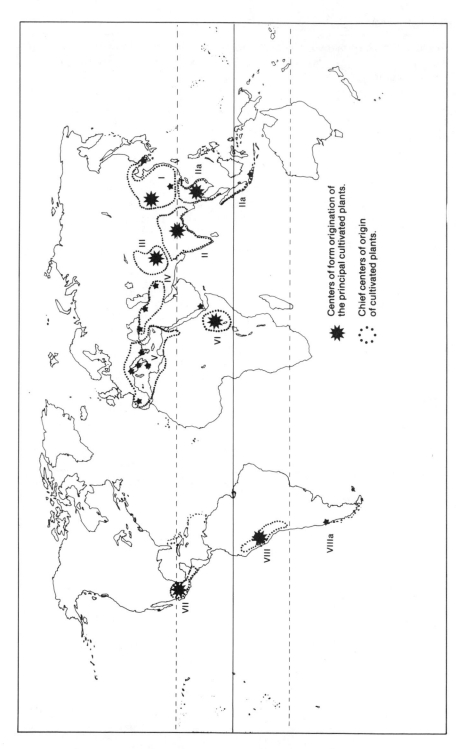

Fig. 3.1 Vavilov's world centers of origin of cultivated plants. (Vavilov, 1951.) Stars indicate centers of form origination of the principal cultivated plants; dotted areas indicate chief centers of origin of cultivated plants.

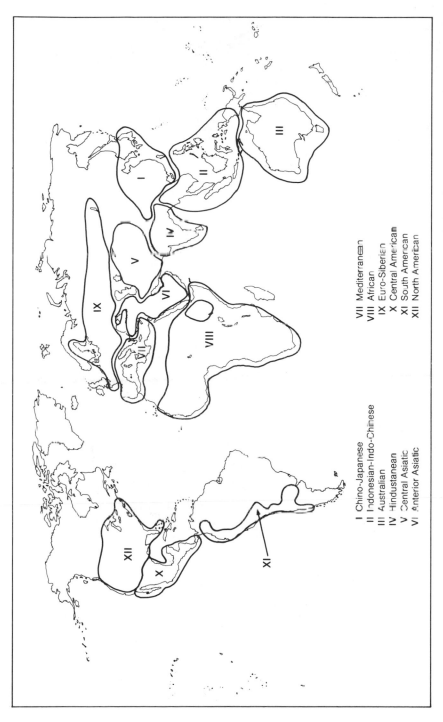

Fig. 3.2 Zhukovsky's gene megacenters of cultivated plants (Zhukovsky, 1975.)

I Chino-Japanese
II Indonesian-Indo-Chinese
III Australian
IV Hindustanean
V Central Asiatic
VI Anterior Asiatic

VII Mediterranean
VIII African
IX Euro-Siberian
X Central American
XI South American
XII North American

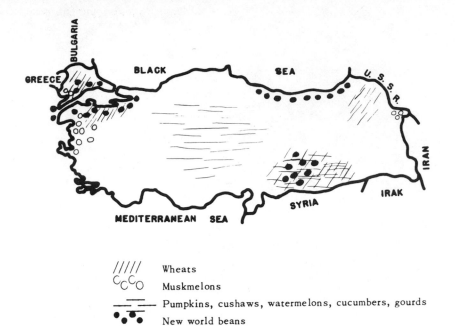

/////	Wheats
$C_C^C_O$	Muskmelons
———	Pumpkins, cushaws, watermelons, cucumbers, gourds
•ₑ•	New world beans

Fig. 3.3 Harlan's Turkish gene microcenters.

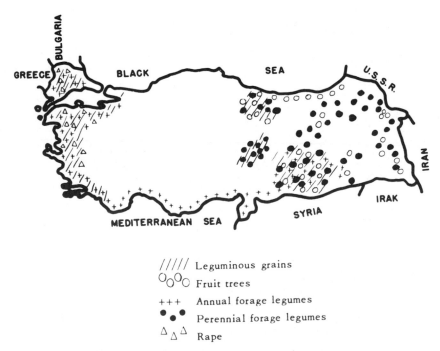

/////	Leguminous grains
$O_O^O_O$	Fruit trees
+++	Annual forage legumes
•ₑ•	Perennial forage legumes
△ △ △	Rape

Fig. 3.4 Harlan's additional Turkish gene microcenters.

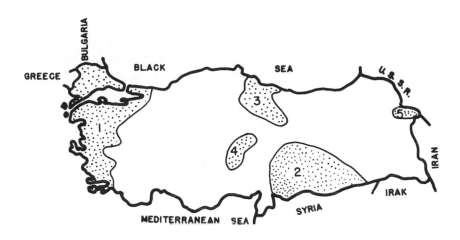

Region 1. Wheats, muskmelons, rape, beans, lentils, chickpeas, broadbeans and
         annual forage legumes (vetches, lupines, clovers).
Region 2. Wheats, tree fruits, grapes, pumpkins, cushaws, watermelons, cucum-
         bers, gourds, beans, lentils, chickpeas, broadbeans and both annual
         and perennial forage legumes.
Region 3. Fruit trees, beans, lentils, broadbeans and forage legumes.
Region 4. Fruit trees, grapes, beans, lentils, chickpeas, broadbeans and forage
         legumes.
Region 5. Fruit trees, muskmelons and forage legumes.

Fig. 3.5   Areas of greatest crop diversity and varietal wealth in Turkey,
according to J. R. Harlan. (Figs. 3.3, 3.4, and 3.5 reprinted from J.
R. Harlan, 1951, *American Naturalist* 85: 97 103, by permission of
The University of Chicago Press. Copyright 1951 by The University
of Chicago.)

Returning now to Vavilov's detailed methods for studying the
origin of a cultivated plant, the following approaches are suggested
by him:

1. Differentiate the plant into specific and infraspecific taxa using
   morphological and genetic criteria.
2. Determine as far as possible the area where such species and
   groups grew in remoter times when travel was restricted.
3. Establish the distribution of genetic diversity and determine the
   geographical centers where this diversity is greatest, especially
   those centers with endemic forms and endemic characters.

4. Determine the centers where the diversity of genetically allied species is concentrated.
5. As a final step, check these centers with the areas of concentration of the nearest wild relatives, which in some instances may belong to the same Linnaean species.
6. When all the botanical information has been gathered together, then archaeological, historical, and linguistic data can be used to help deepen and define our knowledge of the crop plant's origin.
7. Finally, the centers of origin of a group of cultivated plants may also be those of some of their specialized parasites.

F. Bakhteev (1979, personal communication) states that when Vavilov postulated the centers, he attached extreme importance to the time and place of the origin of ancient civilizations because he did not believe that any cultivated plant could originate outside those areas. Vavilov (1926) also postulated that dominant alleles were to be found in the center of origin of a crop plant and recessive alleles toward the periphery. This has since been questioned, but, at least as a broad generalization, it seems to be valid for certain crops, such as potatoes.

The Law of Homologous Series

One of Vavilov's first generalizations concerning the distribution of crop-plant variation was what he described as "geographical regularities in the forms of cultivated plants" (Vavilov 1922, 1926). By this he meant that a similar variation in two or more unrelated crops could be observed in a given area. Thus nonligulate rye and wheat could be found together in Bokhara and naked-grained forms of barley, oats, and millet in China. In addition, he pointed out the well-marked differences between the Mediterranean and the south Asian races of wheat, barley, flax, peas, lentils, broad beans, chickpeas, and castor oil plants. The Mediterranean forms have larger fruits, seeds, and flowers than the Asiatic ones. The same kind of differences can also be observed between the *Phaseolus* species of the New and Old Worlds.

To systematize these examples of parallelism, Vavilov established what he called the Law of Homologous Series, which he claimed could also have useful predictive value.

Briefly, the Law of Homologous Series states that similar variations can be found in unrelated crops in the same geographical
area. Thus, if in a given area a character was known for a certain
crop but not another, one could nevertheless predict that a similar
variant might eventually be found for that second crop. This makes
biological sense, especially when one is looking for disease
resistance, because similar strategies may have evolved in different
species in response to various races of a disease-causing organism
found in a particular area. This has been most valuable in my own
experience with late blight (*Phytophthora infestans*) in the potato;
various types of resistance to late blight can be found in unrelated
species in Mexico. The law also applies, for instance, to resistance
to potato-cyst nematodes; resistance to a number of races of these
organisms is found in a range of widely differing potato species in
the central Andes of Peru, Bolivia, and northwestern Argentina (see
Fig. 3.6).

There is therefore no doubt that such parallel evolution occurs,
but it might have come about for several different reasons, depending on which selection pressures were acting on the crops of a
given area. Also, perhaps such parallelism should more accurately
be described as analogous, rather than homologous, since different
genetic loci are certainly involved. Various Russian authors have
taken up this point, among them Kupzov (1959), who gives a series
of very useful examples of tall and short ecotypes, early and late
maturing forms, and several other groups of characters. He sees
parallelism as similar mutations occurring in related species,
possibly on identical loci, and also as the evolution of different
adaptive gene complexes that result in similar phenotypes. Selection pressures can of course be climatic, edaphic, or biotic.

Primary and Secondary Crops

A final point to be considered in evaluating Vavilov's contribution to crop origins and evolution is the distinction he made between primary and secondary crops. He is often credited with being
the first to establish this hypothesis, though in reality such credit
must go to Engelbrecht (1916), a plant geographer, as de Candolle
was in the previous century. Engelbrecht pointed out that most
crops in earlier times had attendant weeds, belonging to different

Fig. 3.6 Distribution of certain potato pest- and pathogen-resistant genes. (Hawkes, 1958.)

species and even genera, associated with them and mimicking very closely such features as seed size and maturity time. They were therefore harvested and threshed under the same conditions as the crop. One can readily see that ruderal plants, that is, those exhibiting ecological weediness, would be attracted to the fields that man prepared for his crops. Many such weeds would have been eliminated, but any mutations that tended to change seed size and shape, as well as maturity time, toward that of the crop itself would have been unconsciously selected for. Well-known mimetic weeds are *Camelina sativa* subsp. *alyssum* in flax and *Bromus secalinus* in wheat.

Engelbrecht goes on to give examples of attendant weeds becoming the actual crops when the "host species" is taken by man into regions that are less suitable for it but more suitable for its weeds. In fact, he describes what I like to call an "agrovicariad series" for rice, which, in regions too dry for it, is replaced by finger millet, *Eleusine coracana*, to be followed in poorer soils by the little millet, *Panicum miliare*, and in even poorer soils by the small koda millet, *Paspalum scrobiculatum*. He mentions other examples of agrovicariads, such as the replacement of *Sorghum* by *Pennisetum americanum* (=*typhoideum*) in dryer regions of India, of *Setaria viridis* by *Panicum miliaceum*, and of barley and wheat by oats and rye. Engelbrecht claims that several other domesticated plants are secondary crops, including *Cicer arietinum* in cultivations of *Vicia faba*, *Fagopyrum tataricum* in *F. esculentum*, and other, less certain examples.

Vavilov (1926) expanded and systematized this hypothesis by designating as "primary" the ancient crops known only as cultivated plants. Examples of primary crops are wheat, barley, rice, soybean, flax, and cotton. He defined secondary crops as those that began as weeds of primary crops and generally became cultivated at a much later stage, adjusting to the growth of the primary crops and mimicking them in a number of physiological and morphological characters through the effect of unconscious artificial selection. In contrast to such plants as *Bromus secalinus* mentioned above, which never passed beyond the weed stage, these one-time weeds really became crops in their own right. Vavilov gives as examples rye (*Secale cereale*), various species of oats (*Avena*), *Camelina sativa* (subsp. *sativa*), *Eruca sativa*, *Spergula arvensis* var. *maxima* (but

surely this is never more than a weed?), *Fagopyrum tataricum,
Abutilon theophrasti, Coriandrum sativum,* and several kinds of
vetches (see Table 3.2).

As the primary crops were taken into cooler regions, either further north or at higher altitudes, or, in other cases, into drier
regions, they could not adapt to such conditions very well, although
the weeds were able to thrive better, until finally the weed became
the crop and the crop the weed (see Fig. 3.7).

Similarly, I have postulated that the tomato *Lycopersicon
esculentum* is also a secondary crop (Hawkes, 1969), since it apparently spread from its point of origin as a species in Peru north-
ward and eastward throughout the tropics of the New World as a
weed of maize and *Phaseolus* beans. It was then brought into
cultivation in Mexico, and possibly also in some other regions,
where there is a tremendous range of tomato fruit-types that are
quite unknown in other parts of the world.

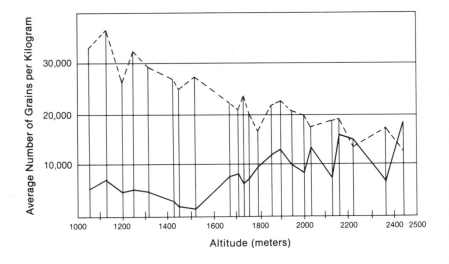

Fig. 3.7 Changes in the proportion of rye and wheat, when ascending from
the lower to the upper zones in mountainous Zeravshan. Horizontal axis: altitude in meters. Vertical axis: average number of grains
per kilogram of wheat - - - - -, rye ———. Note beginnings of crop-
weed reversal from about 2200 m upward. (From Darlington, 1973,
after Batyrenko, 1926.)

Table 3.2 Origins of crops from weeds.

Primary Crop	Secondary Crop	Origin as Weed
Triticum vulgare	Secale cereale	Southwestern Asia
Hordeum vulgare and Triticum dicoccum	Avena sativa	Europe and Western Asia
Linum usitatissimum	Eruca sativa	Central Asia
	Camelina sativa	Transcaucasia
	Spergula linicola	Transcaucasia
	Brassica campestris	Transcaucasia
Fagopyrum esculentum	F. tataricum	Altai
Cereals	Vicia sativa, etc	Southwestern Asia
	Pisum arvense	
	Coriandrum sativum	Transcaucasia
	Cephalaria syriaca	Asia Minor
Various crops	Cucumis trigonus	Turkestan
	Abutilon avicennae	Mediterranean to China

Source: From Darlington, 1973. Derived from the observations of Engelbrecht, 1916, and Vavilov, 1926; compare Schiemann, 1943.

Vavilov emphasized the importance of weed races of crops not only because of their theoretical interest but also because, as Harlan (1965) and others have pointed out, such weeds act as reservoirs of variability, representing rapidly evolving races that are able to exchange genes with the crop through occasional bursts of hybridization. They are thus of great importance to the plant breeder in his search for valuable genetic variation. Thus, Vavilov, who stressed that wild and weedy types taxonomically close to the cultigens formed one ecological group with them, set an example in his work with weeds that many other breeders have followed.

Modifications and Criticisms of Vavilov's Gene Center Theory

Even as early as 1926 Vavilov clearly recognized that the centers of botanical diversity of certain crops are not always their centers of origin. He therefore tried to distinguish between primary centers of diversity which were thus centers of origin, and secondary centers of diversity which were not centers of origin for the crops concerned. However, since he did not consider that the distribution of related wild species was as important as centers of crop diversity in deciding on the point of origin of a crop, he made several mistakes in judging which centers were primary and which secondary for the crops in question.

As Zohary (1969) points out, in most of Vavilov's publications the centers of diversity are referred to as centers of origin. Yet, even though each center is the place where *some* crops originated, it most certainly is not a center of origin for *all* the crop plants Vavilov listed for it. Zohary also made the important point, with which all plant evolutionists would agree, that biological entities accumulate variations at different rates in different places. Even though mutation rates *may* be more or less constant, selection pressures are obviously going to differ enormously from place to place so that the end results may be that in regions with a very wide range of variation, a crop may build up more variation over a shorter period than in other areas of more constant selective pressures. On the other hand, if selection pressures in a particular area are very intense, the crop plant's diversity will be greatly diminished.

Schiemann (1939, 1943, 1951), whose work made a very substantial contribution to our knowledge of cultivated plant origins and evolution, pointed out difficulties with Vavilov's gene-center theory in relation to the Ethiopian and to the central Asian centers, which Vavilov claimed were the centers of origin of durum wheats and barley, and of hexaploid bread wheats, respectively. Other crops demonstrate similar flaws in the theory, because even though the diversity of the crops concerned is very great, none of the wild progenitors is present in, or even found close by, the centers. Schiemann called such areas "accumulation centers," by which she meant that genetic variation had accumulated in them over the millennia, even though the crops did not originate in them.

Other writers have not been so cautious, so that some, such as Brücher (1969), have doubted whether the gene-center theory had any scientific basis whatever. This view is an extreme one and has been criticized by Kupzov (1976) and others, who mention the reasons for the historical development of gene centers, such as variable ecological conditions, antiquity of cultivation, and weak selection pressures. Harlan (1975) also contests Brücher's view by stating that some crops have gene centers and others do not. The fact remains, however, that there are many centers or regions where the diversity of a number of crops coincides.

In fact, very few authorities would deny that variation is more intense in some areas of the world than in others. Furthermore, by and large, the regions of ancient civilizations throughout the world are regions where variations have built up. It is in the matter of detail and judgment where the major criticisms lie.

Some critics have pointed out that centers 2 (India), 3 (Central Asia), 4 (the Near East), and 5 (the Mediterranean) are confluent and should be thought of as a continuous band. However, these centers are of value in delimiting regions of crop diversity and agroecological adaptation. Other workers (see Harlan, 1971) have claimed that certain centers (Brazil, Southeast Asia, and the Mediterranean, for example) are too diffuse and are not really centers, in the usual meaning of that word, at all. This criticism is perhaps partly due to a misconception by non-Russian speakers of the exact meaning of the Russian texts. The starred locations on Vavilov's map (Vavilov, 1935), for instance, are stated to be "Centers of Form Origination," while the dotted lines delimit areas called "Chief Centers of Origin." The Mediterranean region has five of these stars, the Near East three, China three also, and Ethiopia (including the southwestern corner of Arabia) has two. We are thus shown general areas ("centers") with smaller centers, where many new forms originated, lying within them. It was perhaps the starred centers that Zhukovsky (1970) thought of as gene microcenters, or actual points of origins of the crops. I was fortunate enough to have known both Vavilov and Zhukovsky personally; yet, unfortunately, I never thought then to discuss such issues with them.

Other critics of Vavilov, such as Kuckuck (1962), have not been able to find dominant alleles in the center and recessives in the periphery of distribution (e.g. in wheats and sorghum). As I said, Vavilov's hypothesis seems to work for potatoes but not for all crops.

Perhaps the most serious criticism of the gene center theory has been advanced by Harlan (1971). In a paper entitled "Agricultural Origins: Centers and Noncenters," he postulated only three true "centers," each with a more-or-less connected but very large and diffuse "noncenter" (see Figs. 3.8, 3.9). Thus, progressing from east to

Fig. 3.8 Centers and noncenters of agricultural origins: A1, Near East center; A2, African noncenter; B1, northern Chinese center; B2, SouthEast Asian and South Pacific noncenter; C1, Meso-American center; C2, South American noncenter. (Harlan, 1971; copyright 1971 by the American Association for the Advancement of Science.)

west we have, according to Harlan, a small northern Chinese centre (B1) and a Southeast Asian and South Pacific noncenter (B2). Further west we have the Near East center (A1) and an African noncenter (A2). Finally, in the New World, Harlan distinguishes a Meso-American center (C1) and a South American noncenter (C2).

While Harlan's comments are intriguing and are purposely designed to shake up accepted thinking, I believe his theory of centers and noncenters is somewhat rigid and too formal. We are to some extent all involved with a problem of semantics. How large can a "center" be before it is obviously not a center at all, but an

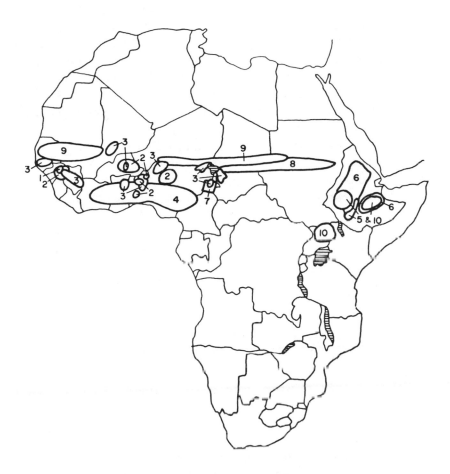

Fig. 3.9 Probable areas of domestication of selected African crops: 1, *Brachiaria deflexa*; 2, *Digitaria exilis* and *Digitaria iburua*; 3, *Oryza glaberrima*; 4, *Dioscorea rotundata*; 5, *Musa ensete* and *Guizotia abyssinica*; 6, *Eragrostis tef*; 7, *Voandzeia* and *Kerstingiella*; 8, *Sorghum bicolor*; 9, *Pennisetum americanum*; 10, *Eleusine coracana*. (Harlan, 1971; copyright 1971 by the American Association for the Advancement of Science.)

area or a region? There is also a problem of distinguishing between places where agriculture originated (Harlan's centers A1, B1, and C1) and places where many other cultivated plants were domesticated. Obviously, a few cultigens, perhaps not more than a dozen in total, in these three centers, were the plants that were involved in the beginnings of agriculture. After this, secondary weed crops became established, while later still, people began to cultivate other plants consciously. However, by that time the original crops had extended beyond their first, nuclear areas.

In his 1975 paper, Harlan deals with individual crops, recognizing that some are endemic only to a very small area, others are monocentric, still others are oligocentric, and certain crops, such as sorghum, are noncentric. He thinks that noncentric patterns arise when the wild progenitors are widely dispersed. It does seem, too, that secondary crops that arose after going through a weed stage in different places also seem to be noncentric. The examples of rye and oats certainly support this idea. Indeed, sorghum, the clearest example of a noncentric crop mentioned by Harlan, may also be a secondary crop according to some authorities.

The centers Harlan postulated (1971) had already been discussed in a simpler form by Darlington (1956, 1963, 1973), who speaks of the Near Eastern and the Mexican areas as nuclear centers, from which agriculture would have spread throughout the Old World and the New, respectively. Sauer (1952) had a similar idea, though his centers, or "hearths," were Southeast Asia and Central America. These nuclear centers were differentiated, in Darlington's and Harlan's thinking, from the centers of genetic diversity, of which Darlington, in fact, proposed twelve (Darlington and Janaki Ammal, 1945). Some of these, such as the Brazilian and the United States centers, have been criticized because they include very few native cultigens. Yet these centers were not Vavilov's creations at all.

Nuclear Centers and Regions of Diversity

It is clear that our knowledge and understanding of crop plant diversity has increased considerably during the years since Vavilov's death. The ideas of Sauer, Kupzov, Darlington, Harlan, and others have added understanding to his concepts, which undoubtedly Vavilov himself would have modified had he lived. Much of the confusion seems to have arisen when the nuclear centers of agricultural origins were confused with the areas of evolution and diversity of crop plants other than those first cultivated when agriculture began.

To clarify these issues, I have put forward an alternative scheme, summarized in Table 3.3. This concept distinguishes the *nuclear centers* of agricultural origins from the *regions of diversity* which developed later when farming had spread out from the nuclear areas in which it originated. Certain outlying *minor centers*, probably of more recent origin, can also be distinguished.

Nuclear Centers

The nuclear centers are the places where agriculture first began, or is believed to have done so:

A. Northern China (the loess regions north of the Yellow River)
B. The Near East (Fertile Crescent)
C. Southern Mexico (from Tehuacán southward)
D. Central to southern Peru (the Andes, the eastern Andean slopes, and the coastal belt).

Table 3.3 Nuclear centers and regions of diversity of domesticated plants.

Nuclear Centers	Regions of Diversity		Outlying Minor Centers	
A. Northern China	I.	China	1.	Japan
	II.	India	2.	New Guinea
	III.	Southeast Asia	3.	Solomon Islands, Fiji, and South Pacific
B. The Near East	IV.	Central Asia	4.	Northwestern Europe
	V.	The Near East		
	VI.	The Mediterranean		
	VII.	Ethiopia		
	VIII.	West Africa		
C. Southern Mexico	IX.	Meso-America	5.	United States, Canada
			6.	The Caribbean
D. Central to southern Peru	X.	Northern Andes (Venezuela to Bolivia	7.	Southern Chile
			8.	Brazil

Regions of diversity

For historical reasons I would have liked to retain the word *center*, but *region* is really more accurate. Regions of diversity are the areas into which the domesticated plants spread from the nuclear centers and in which additional cultigens arose, both by unconscious and by conscious selection processes. The regions equate with Vavilov's centers fairly well (Vavilov, 1935, 1951), but it is necessary to modify some names slightly. Regions I–III are associated mainly with the northern Chinese (A) and also with the Near Eastern nuclear center (B). Regions IV–VII are associated mainly with the Near Eastern nuclear center (B). Region VIII is probably related to the Near Eastern nuclear center (B) through Ethiopia. Region IX is related to the southern Mexican nuclear center (C). The northern Andean region, comprising Venezuela, Colombia, Ecuador, Peru, Bolivia, and adjacent lowlands, is related to the central Peruvian nuclear center (D).

Minor centers

There are a number of minor centers, probably of more recent origin, which I have purposely avoided terming "microcenters," so as not to confuse them with those of Zhukovsky and Harlan. These are places where only a few crops, sometimes not more than one or two, seem to have originated. Examples are: Japan (origin of *Vigna angularis*), New Guinea (sugar cane), Solomon Islands to Fiji (Fe'i bananas), northwestern Europe (*Avena strigosa, Secale cereale, Ribes* species, *Rubus* species), Chile (*Bromus mango, Madia sativa*), Brazil (*Manihot esculenta, Ananas comosus*), the United States (*Helianthus annuus, H. tuberosus*). Such crops may have arisen through knowledge gained by cultural diffusion from adjacent regions.

This scheme is, of course, tentative. By distinguishing the nuclear centers of agricultural origins from Vavilov's broader "centers," I have tried to combine his views with those of Darlington, Harlan, and others, adding some ideas of my own. We obviously need far more archaeological data for Africa, India, and Southeast Asia before we can be certain about nuclear centers for these areas. However, we can relate the nuclear centers about which we are reasonably certain to the regions of diversity, which are more or less equivalent to Vavilov's centers of diversity.

Conclusion

Clearly, the story is not yet complete. The originally high levels of variation in the regions of diversity are already diminishing through genetic erosion. We have come a long way from Vavilov's concept that every region, or center of diversity, was at the same time a center of origin of all the crops that constituted it. The picture is more complex, as Harlan (1975), Kupzov (1965), and others have shown. Yet the fact remains that without Vavilov's brilliantly intuitive hypotheses, our knowledge of the diversity of crop plants and their origins would never have led us to the understanding that modern plant breeding demands.

We can do no better than to end this chapter with a quotation from F. Bakhteev (1979, personal communication), who has to a considerable extent carried on in Vavilov's traditions: "Vavilov's centers of origin have already done their work in that they have enabled collectors to direct their efforts to those geographical areas of the earth where it was still possible to find the maximum amount of very old endemic botanical material being cultivated by man."

4

The Evidence of Crop Plant Diversity

Plants have spread from their nuclear centers, or other regions where they were first domesticated, into areas where they diversified because of differences in the climate, altitude, day-length, soils, and farming practices. Over much of these areas, such crops as hemp, potatoes, wheat, barley, and sorghum have been accompanied by closely related races of weeds with which they have exchanged genes, adding to their mutual diversity.

The Accumulation of Diversity

The limited flow, or introgression, as it is called, of genes from related wild and weedy species into the cultigen has undoubtedly been an extremely important phenomenon during the evolution of cultivated plants under domestication. Harlan (1970) draws attention to the alternating cycles of hybridization and differentiation in various crops and their attendant weed races. Gene flow is restricted enough to prevent the total disintegration of distinct crop and weed species but flexible enough to allow cycles of exchange of genes between the two entities. Genetic buffering of the effects of gene flow may be weak, as it is in barley, but can be somewhat stronger in crops such as maize, and even stronger in the polyploid crops such as wheat, potatoes, and sugar cane.

Zohary (1970) believes even more than Harlan that introgression is extremely important in the evolution of a crop plant such as, for example, the sunflower *Helianthus annuus*, which has picked up genes in various places and from several different species as it was being domesticated throughout its whole area of distribution (see Heiser, 1955). A similar situation has been described for sorghum by Doggett (1965). In such complex cases, conventional taxonomy becomes almost meaningless.

In many instances whole genomes have been incorporated into a plant by polyploidy. We are far from knowing all the details of these processes, and perhaps the riddle may never be solved with certainty for some plants. Where we do possess fairly clear evidence, there seems to have been a marked extension of the range of adaptation of the original diploid crop. We have only to compare the restricted geographical range of diploid wheats with the very much wider range of tetraploid and hexaploid species which possess genomes of the wild grass genus *Aegilops*. Similarly, the diploid cultivated potatoes are more geographically and ecologically restricted, on the whole, than are the tetraploids.

Zohary (1970) and Swaminathan (1970) point out several cases of intricate polyploid complexes where diploid "pillars" support a superstructure of intricate polyploid complexes with continuous variation, combining and fusing the separate gene pools found among the diploids. A few cases of this type of polyploidy have been studied, such as in *Dactylis* (Stebbins and Zohary, 1959), but a number of others probably exist. Studies of morphophysiological variability demonstrate that cultivated plants have also differentiated into geographical and ecological races, known as agroecotypes, not only in their Vavilovian regions of diversity but also in the other areas into which they were introduced subsequent to the European voyages of discovery in the fifteenth and sixteenth centuries. According to Hutchinson (1965, chapter 8), the differentiation has been rapid, and the nature of the sample of the population from which the original supply of seed was taken has almost always left its effect on the new race. New characters also arise in response to the new selection pressures imposed on the crop in its new environment.

Vavilov (1957) thought that plant introduction could be made much more effective if one could characterize the main agroecological regions of the world. This would thus enable one to introduce material of the correct agroecological adaptation into a plant breeding program in another geographical area. As Vavilov said, "The final aim of our research was to reveal the selection value of the variety of material of different regions with the aim of applying these findings in various areas of the USSR." Thus the study of agroecological regions would provide "a path for further work by the plant breeder" (1957, p.85).

The inheritance of blocks of genes that allow a plant to adapt to particular climatic and edaphic conditions has been a matter of some controversy. Undoubtedly, strains of the crops evolving over long periods of time known as land races and the ancient or primitive forms of cultivated species have through natural and artificial selection become well adapted to the conditions under which they are grown. Whether such "adaptive complexes" can be inherited in a simple way is not so certain. Vavilov's work, however, which called attention to crop materials already adapted to various agroecological conditions is undoubtedly of great value. Even if not every adaptive complex remained intact during the generations of breeding and selection, at least some qualities of adaptation and disease resistance would stand a good chance of being inherited.

In addition to this, the study of the distribution areas of crops (Kupzov, 1965) can tell us a great deal about their present range of adaptation in relation to that of the wild species from which they were derived. Vavilov (1957) and Hartley (1970) have shown also that detailed studies of climatic patterns can provide a key to the probable success that breeders may hope to attain in widening the adaptive range of the crop. Hartley thus concludes, for example, that the prospects for developing rice cultivars that can resist cold are better than those for developing varieties resistant to drought, and breeders would likely have better success with barley varieties adapted to cool, dry regions than those adapted to humid, tropical ones.

Most breeders, and even knowledgeable laymen, would agree with these conclusions. Nevertheless, screening of rice for drought resistance is being considered seriously by scientists at the International Rice Research Institute (IRRI) (see Chang, Loresto, and Tagumpay, 1974). Sprague and Finlay from the International Maize and Wheat Improvement Center (CIMMYT) are even more optimistic: "Increasing evidence suggests that, if there is moisture and solar energy, the breeder can adapt any species to any environment — given time and access to a wide range of genetic variability" (Sprague and Finlay, 1976). Although this seems, even in the present age of genetic engineering, a little *too* optimistic, one can clearly see that in the last decade vast strides have been made or are contemplated in plant-breeding research. Perhaps the operative phrase here is "time and a wide range of genetic variability" — variability that seems more feasible now that exploration and evaluation of genetic variability in crops is taking place.

In the circumstances of domestication, then, exposure of plants to different environments and to the varying selection pressures resulting from the changing techniques of farming have caused crop plants to evolve very rapidly indeed. They have also formed natural hybrids with related wild species under conditions and to a degree that would not have occurred at all if agriculture had not taken place. Resistance to the diseases and pests that attack them has also developed in species of cultivated plants. Yet, the increase in numbers of individuals and the fact that they have been cultivated in close proximity have provided conditions nearly ideal for the pathogens. With continual genetic change in the crops, followed by accompanying changes in the pathogens, a remarkably complex picture has built up.

Vavilov noted this fact, and believed that the center of diversity of the pathogens generally coincided with the center of diversity, and therefore, according to him, the center of origin, of the crop. This is true in many, but not all, instances. In certain cases the parasite has evolved in company with wild species related to but not originally in contact with the crop. Once the crop spreads into the distribution area of the parasite, it immediately succumbs to it, as, for example, *Phytophthora infestans* in Mexico, and the Colorado beetle in the southwestern United States. The wild species in these areas had built up various types of resistance, but the potato crop had not. Another situation also exists, for example, in Ethiopia, where barleys highly resistant to the yellow dwarf virus disease are found (Qualset, 1975). Yet barley did not originate as a crop in this region, nor are any of its related wild species found there. Furthermore, Ethiopia is the only region where such resistance exists. We must therefore show caution in applying such hypotheses as

Vavilov's, because although they sound satisfying and logical, only the facts will demonstrate whether they are universally true or not.

Diversity within Crops and Wild Species

For a description of diversity in crop plants, we must again turn first to Vavilov, particularly to his monumental work entitled *World Resources of Cereals, Leguminous Seed Crops and Flax and Their Utilization in Breeding*, prepared by 1940 but published only in 1957, posthumously. This was clearly the first attempt to show the valuable diversity then available in a series of crops and to relate the diversity to the climate, soil, and farming practices of the regions where the crops were grown. His notes on the resistance of crops to pests and diseases and on the adaptation of local agroecotypes make particularly valuable reading for the plant breeder. The adaptive variation of these old land races and primitive forms of crop plants in their centers of diversity was stressed also by Bennett (1970a), who contrasted these materials with the genetically much more uniform ones grown in the highly developed countries. She also pointed out that much of the variation of the primitive forms and wild species is quantitative, even though some genes of major effect can also be seen and are of considerable importance.

A further study of the variation in the crops available to breeders was provided by Frankel (1973), in which he commissioned studies of a wide range of crops growing in different regions of the world. In a later publication (Frankel and Soule, 1981) he concluded (p. 223) that "there is good evidence, from direct observation and from germplasm collections, of extensive diversity between and within land races, although their genetic structure has not been extensively studied; what evidence we have comes mainly from studies of wild relatives of crop species."

To study the amount of genetic diversity in a species where most of it can be understood only through the use of quantitative methods is not an easy task, and it is one that, for obvious reasons, can only be tackled by the population geneticist. Allard (1970a) points out that each species contains millions, or even hundreds of millions, of variants, but at the same time, he infers that diversity is not spread evenly throughout the distribution area; it is more concentrated in areas of high climatic and ecological diversity and less so in ecologically uniform regions. This conclusion agrees with Vavilov's views on cultivated plants, as we have seen. Nevertheless, diversity in crop plants is conditioned not only by geographical, climatic, and edaphic features but also by cultural and ethnic differences of the peoples who grow them (Kupzov, 1965) — their farming practices, their historical traditions, their religious and cultural beliefs, and their tribal boundaries.

Detailed Studies of Large Collections

Careful analyses of the genetic diversity of crop plants and their wild relatives are very much a phenomenon of the 1970s and 1980s. These have relied on numerical studies of morphological characters and those biochemical features that can be analyzed fairly easily with the more sophisticated techniques now available. For example, Jeswani, Murty, and Mehra (1970) used multivariate analysis to study morphological features of a collection of flax (*Linum usitatissimum*) that exhibited much phenotypic diversity. There were seven groups: Afghan, European, Russian, Indian, North American, Argentinian, and Australian. Although the European group was not very different from the Russian, American, and Australian material, the Indian group differed from all others very markedly; even the Afghan group was not as close to the Indian group as it was to the others. Within each group, and particularly within the Indian and Afghan groups, considerable diversity for a range of characters was seen. This is taken as evidence that the Indian group was of polyphyletic origin.

Infraspecific divergence in rice was dealt with by Jawahar Ram and Panwar (1970), also using multivariate analysis of morphometric and phenological features. The methods were able to distinguish the differences between the *indica* and *japonica* races; between early-, medium-, and late-maturing groups; and between varieties from China, Japan, and Taiwan, and the Indian hills and plains. Here was a strong indication of clear geographical diversity in rice.

The associations of morphological characters with disease resistance were shown by Ashri (1971) for safflower (*Carthamus tinctorius*). Twenty morphological and phenological traits were analyzed, and resistance to disease was found to be linked not only to some of the morphological characters but also to the plant's place of origin. Presumably, the correlation of disease resistance with locality has resulted from the different selection pressures within each region. This fact is frequently assumed in general discussions, but it is gratifying to find it clearly demonstrated.

The phenotypic diversity of a collection of more than 3,000 varieties of *Triticum durum* was examined by Jain and others (1975), who again analyzed morphological characters. Clear indications of great diversity in this wheat were seen especially in varieties from Ethiopia and Portugal, with varieties from Italy, Hungary, Greece, Poland, Cyprus, India, Tunisia, and Egypt also demonstrating a wide range of differences. On the whole, it was concluded that great diversity in this wheat could still be seen in the Mediterranean region and in Ethiopia, thus agreeing in broad terms with what Vavilov had written some 50 years earlier.

A somewhat complementary study was carried out by Porceddu (1976) on a collection of 2,400 samples (accessions) of *durum* wheat that were scored for six agronomic characters and that originally came from many countries. Multivariate analyses showed that Mediterranean accessions were very similar, no doubt because of old trade connections within the area; these accessions showed many similarities to samples from some Near Eastern countries. Rather more distinct were varieties from the Soviet Union and Middle Eastern countries.

An interesting analysis of wheat materials collected in Nepal by Witcombe and Rao (1976), using 39 plant characters, indicated that there were five main genecological regions that were associated with altitude but influenced also by the amount of gene flow within and between the regions. In a later study on wheat and barley from Nepal and Pakistan, Witcombe and Gilani (1979) came to the conclusion that the diversity of crops within these regions was not really greater than that to be found outside them.

Biochemical Analyses

Electrophoretic and chromatographic techniques that enable the experimenter to undertake mass screenings for enzyme protein, and flavonoid patterns have been used during the last decade with considerable success in the study of genetic variation in populations and in species. A very popular crop for these studies has been barley, to some extent because of the enigmatic nature of its origin. Allard, Kahler, and Weir (1971), for example, studying esterase A, B, and C loci, found that very many varieties of barley were polymorphic for one or more of the three loci and that clinal patterns across the Eurasian land mass could be discerned from east to west. Brown, Nevo, and Zohary (1977) reported on the widespread occurrence of co adapted combinations of alleles at four esterase loci in wild barley (*Hordeum spontaneum*) from Israel. This work was further reported on by Nevo, Brown, and Zohary (1979), who studied 1,179 individuals in 28 populations of wild barley covering the entire ecological range in Israel. As was to be expected, it was found that the species was highly polymorphic in its allozyme variation and that clinal, regional, and local patterns were correlated with climate and soil. This suggests that natural selection is of great importance in this wild species.

Nakagahra, Akihama, and Hayashi (1975) have carried out interesting studies on esterase isozymes with leaves of 776 accessions of Asian rice. Each isozyme differed in its frequency of occurrence in each of the eight areas from Sri Lanka to Japan, and many bands showed a clear geographical cline, with simple patterns occurring both toward the north and south. On the other hand, the zymogram patterns were much more widely varied in an area that included Nepal, Bhutan, Assam, Burma, Vietnam, and Yunan (China). (See Fig. 4.1.) This area was postulated as the center of genetic diversity of rice, and, interestingly enough, it does indeed correspond fairly closely with the proposed center of origin for that crop (Ng and others, 1982).

Flavonoid patterns in barley were studied by Fröst, Holm, and Asker (1975), revealing similarities that gave some indications of possible phylogeny. Patterns A and B were widespread in *Hordeum vulgare,* while pattern C was almost completely confined to Ethiopia. This distinct polymorphism agrees very much with the polymorphisms of isozymes referred to above. A final example of crop plant diversity can be taken from studies of potatoes conducted by Stegemann and Loeschcke (1976), who characterized all the European potato varieties using slab electrophoresis and found that *every one* of them possessed a distinct electropherogram, or

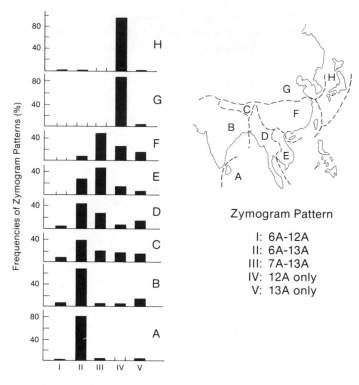

Fig. 4.1 Geographic cline in esterase zymogram patterns of *Oryza sativa* in Asia. (Nakagahra, Akihama, and Hayashi, 1975.)

pattern, of protein lines. This is indeed a remarkable example of genetic diversity in a group of cultivars.

Enough has been said, perhaps, from the few examples I have mentioned, to show that careful analysis can indicate very great genetic differences within cultivated plant species. These differences may be morphological or agronomic or both, and therefore easy to see and comprehend, but they may also be biochemical and verifiable only by sophisticated experimental techniques. Finally, they may relate to pest and disease resistance, and any breeder working on these topics will be able to verify the results amply from his own experience.

In probably all the studies in which a reasonable number of samples bear location data, a clear correlation of diversity with locality and altitude can be observed. This correlation is not surprising, since, as I have already mentioned, we assume that selection pressures are controlling this diversity to a greater or lesser extent. How this control is imposed on isozyme frequencies or flavonoid patterning we do not yet know. The relation of climate to growth, flowering time, and seed maturity is more obvious. Disease resistance can sometimes be explained in terms of its obvious correlation with a high incidence of the pathogen; in other cases we can only assume that there is some other, as-yet-unknown causal relationship. What is quite certain, however, is this: the more techniques we use to study species of cultivated plants, the more diversity we find. Undoubtedly, much of this knowledge can be put to good practical use in the future.

Orchard and Kitchen Gardens as Sources of Crop Plant Diversity

There are some parts of the world, and certain situations within them, where the amount of variation in a crop plant still remains close to what it was in ancient times. These areas are to be found particularly in the tropics, not in tropical plantations but in the small kitchen gardens and orchards around the huts and cottages of poor farmers or herders. Plants grown on tropical plantations show very little diversity. One sees hundreds of hectares of rice, sugar cane, maize, sorghum, rubber, bananas, soybean, cassava, and the like, each a standard genotype that represents the end product of plant breeding. Most of these high-yielding varieties owe their existence to great genetic diversity in the first place — material of high diversity from which they were ultimately selected. If we wish to look at crop plant diversity still more or less in its original form, we must turn to the small plots of the individual farmers who may be growing crop populations in the time-honored manner rather than the standard uniform cultivars.

In his well-known *Plants, Man and Life* (1952), the late Edgar Anderson described in great detail the diversity to be found in such small orchards and gardens, as well as the lack of any apparent uniform pattern to the diversity. He reported, for example, that "in India there is seldom any such thing as a field all of one variety of wheat. The interplanting of various crops is the rule, and frequently actual mixtures are planted and harvested and ground and used together." Later he said, significantly, "If agriculture did begin with dumpheap-orchard gardens, then these conservative areas are growing crops under conditions more closely resembling those of Neolithic times."

Anderson (1952, chapter 9) describes a study he made in Guatemala of an Indian garden (see Figs. 4.2 and 4.3) where the "riotous growth, so luxuriant and so apparently planless" would have led an American or European visitor to suppose that it was deserted. Anderson found that it was anything but planless and was carefully designed to prevent soil erosion and colonization of the plot by unwanted weeds, while retaining moisture and making the best use possible of the available space and soil. The garden was in continuous production, and there was always a large variety of food and condiment plants available. The orchard garden, of about 25 species, is thus an example of the kind of multiple cropping that closely follows the pattern of the natural ecosystems.

Kimber (1973) describes similar systems in Puerto Rico, which she calls dooryard gardens. Being a geographer, she carefully studied the different types, ranging from what she considers to be the most primitive, or "Jibaro garden" (Fig. 4.4), through the "traditional garden" (Fig. 4.5) to the "vernacular garden," and then gardens that are so carefully managed that they are of little interest to the plant evolutionist. The first two types of garden perhaps come close to that described by Anderson, and it is interesting to note that Kimber observes that there has been a "differentiation of species into races and varieties." Unfortunately, she does not list the species grown, but from the diagrams given there seems to be quite a large number.

In Indonesia, I was able to see an example of an orchard garden in central Java (Table 4.1). Together with a colleague from the National Institute of Biology at Bogor and two from Jogjakarta I investigated the total flora of cultivated species in an orchard garden selected at random. This garden contained 45 species of cultivated plants and about 25 more wild ones that were said to be used for medicinal purposes. Not only that, but there was a clearly visible genetic variation within a number of cultivated species such as Colocasia esculenta, Manihot esculenta, and others. As with the garden investigated by Anderson, there was some order underlying the ap-

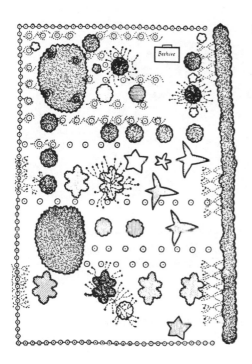

Fig. 4.2 Diagramatic map of an orchard garden in the Indian Village of Santa Lucia, Guatemala. (E. Anderson, *Plants, man, and life,* Berkeley: University of California Press, 1952.)

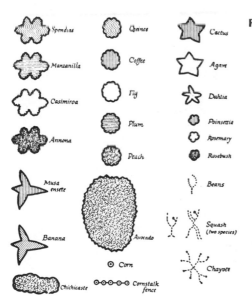

Fig. 4.3 Glyphs representing symbols on Fig. 4.2. The glyphs not only identify the plants as shown in the plan; they indicate by their shapes in what general category the plants belong. Circular glyphs indicate fruit trees (such as plum and peach) of European origin; rounded irregular glyphs indicate fruit trees (such as the manzanilla) which are of American origin. Similarly, dotted lines are for climbing vegetables, small circles for subshrubs, large stars for succulents, and an irregular, wedge-shaped figure for plants in the banana family. The long, irregular, mass at the right-hand side of Fig. 4.2 represents a hedge of "chichicaste," a shrub used by the Mayas. (E. Anderson, *Plants, man, and life,* Berkeley: University of California Press, 1952.)

THE JÍBARO GARDEN

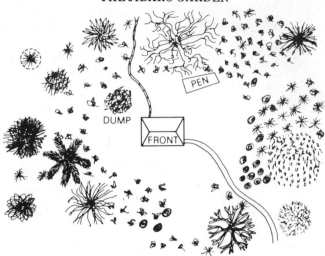

Fig. 4.4   The "Jíbaro garden" in Puerto Rico. (Reprinted from Kimber, *Geographical Review*, vol. 63, 1973, with the permission of the American Geographical Society.)

THE TRADITIONAL GARDEN

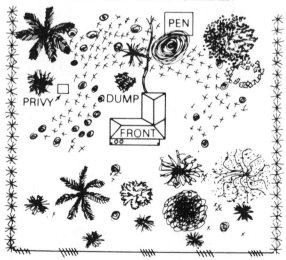

Fig. 4.5   The "traditional garden" in Puerto Rico. (Reprinted from Kimber, *Geographical Review*, vol. 63, 1973, with the permission of the American Geographical Society.)

parent chaos of planting, and the uses of each plant were clearly understood by the owners.

The ecosystem of such orchard gardens closely follows that of the forests themselves: tall trees (coconuts) that form the highest level are interspersed with shorter trees (mostly fruit trees), and shrubs, climbers, and herbs fill up the spaces between the trees, right down to ground level. According to Harris (1969, 1973, 1978), this is an ecologically complex system in which cultivation proceeds by the substitution of selected domesticates for the wild species in equivalent ecological niches, though such a garden cannot be compared too closely with the polycultural swidden plots of a tropical forest. It does, however, simulate the structure and dynamics of the natural ecosystems, for it makes the greatest possible use of every available ecological niche.

It is interesting to note that intraspecific diversity in these gardens is very low and is replaced by interspecific diversity. Again this is similar to the ecosystems of a natural forest, where the number of species is very great, even though each species is represented by only a few individuals. Thus in orchard, kitchen, or dooryard gardening, the populations of each species tend to be dispersed throughout an entire village itself, not limited to an individual plot. This dispersal is even more understandable when one remembers that material for propagation is continually exchanged among villagers.

Such "ecosystems" of orchard and kitchen gardens continue to provide a living laboratory for the evolution of cultivated plants. In this age of monocultures, carefully controlled and weeded, with little chance of natural selection acting on a spectrum of variations within a crop-weed complex, we can nevertheless take heart by knowing that there is still plenty of genetic variation available in the less-important crops. What is worrying, however, is the depletion of genetic variation in the major crops. The need for such variation and the uses to which it is put forms the subject of the next few chapters.

Table 4.1 Species of economic importance cultivated in an orchard garden in Central Java, Indonesia.

Species	Common name
Root and tuber herbs	
Colocasia esculenta	Taro
Impomoea batatas	Sweet potato
Curcuma xanthorrhiza	Temu lawak
Zingiber officinale	Ginger
Amorphophallus campanulatus	Suweg
Maranta arundinacea	Arrowroot
Seed-sown herbs	
Solanum melongena	Eggplant
Cucurbita moschata	Squash
Amaranthus (tricolor ?)	Bayam
Mucuna pruriens	Cowage
Vigna sinensis	Cow pea
Hibiscus cannabinus	Java jute
Crotalaria anagyroides	Orok orok
Capsicum (annuum ?)	Chili pepper
Ocimum basilicum	Selasih
Climbers	
Dioscorea alata	Winged yam
Dioscorea bulbifera	Potato yam
Dioscorea pentaphylla	Ubi pasir
Dioscorea hispida	Asiatic bitter yam
Momordica charantia	Bitter gourd
Shrubs and small trees	
Musa x *sapientium*	Banana
Musa acuminata (seeded)	Banana
Ipomoea fistulosa	("For hedging")
Carica papaya	Pawpaw
Panax fruticosum	Kadongdongan
Jatropha curcas	Purging nut
Taxotrophis macrophylla	—
Gigantochloa atter, forma *nigra*	Black bamboo

Table 4.1 *continued.*

Species	Common name
Trees	
Syzygium cumini	Juwet, jamblang
Syzygium aqueum	Jambu air
Artocarpus heterophylla	Jack fruit
Artocarpus communis	Seeded breadfruit
Moringa oleifera	Horseradish tree
Tamarindus indica	Tamarind
Gnetum gnemon	Melinjo
Cocos nucifera	Coconut
Tectona grandis (young trees)	Teak
Leucaena glauca	Wild tamarind
Morinda citrifolia	Indian mulberry
Citrus maxima	Shaddock
Anacardium occidentale	Cashew nut
Mangifera indica	Mango
Achras sapota	Zapote
Pandanus odorifer	Screw pine
Areca catechu	Botol nut

List made by Mien Rifai and Jack Hawkes, checked in Birmingham by Made Sri Prana.

5

The Value of Diversity to the Breeder

No two plant breeders have completely identical objectives. Yet, despite differences of emphasis here and there, depending on the crop and the climatic, cultural, and economic differences of the country where it is grown, there are underlying similarities in all breeding programs. The basic objectives of most crop plant breeders are: (1) high yields; (2) high quality; (3) high nutritional levels; (4) the maintenance or extension of adaptation to soils and climate; (5) pest and disease resistance. Of course the details of such a list are much more complex and deserve careful examination.

Yield

The breeder must decide what type of yield is desired: more seeds, tubers, and so forth, of the same size, or the same number of seeds or tubers of greater size, or both. Yield is obviously connected with the nutritional value of the plant, since a large yield of produce composed chiefly of water cannot be regarded as better than a smaller yield of produce having more dry matter and better protein. The factors that determine yield are complex, and I do not propose to go into them here in detail. Suffice it to say that all breeding for yield should be based on a thorough understanding of the physiological processes of growth, assimilation, and photoperiodic response. Response to moisture and fertilizer is important to obtain good yields; short-strawed cereals, for example, that can resist lodging and take advantage of high fertilizer applications have been one of the breeding objectives of the "green revolution" wheat and rice varieties, developed at CIMMYT and IRRI, respectively.

Quality

The general palatability, acceptable color, texture, and flavor of raw, cooked, or baked produce, and factors affecting marketing — keeping, storage, ease of handling or packaging — are all qualities that are important no less in developing than in developed countries. Because consumers become accustomed to certain flavors, colors, textures, and so on, breeders must provide these aspects of quality in their new cultivars, even though it would often be easier not to have to do so. Yet, even under conditions of near famine, at least some attention should be paid to the matter of quality as it affects traditional food presentation and requirements.

High nutritional levels

Improving the nutritional value of a crop is of obvious importance because it is the breeder's aim to increase protein in cereals and tuber crops wherever possible. The effective protein content of some of the main food crops is given in Table 5.1. Even more impor-

Table 5.1 The protein contents of staple foods (in percentages).

Food	Calories from protein	Efficiency of protein utilization	Effective protein
Cassava	1.8	50	0.9
Plantain	3.1	50	1.6
Yam	7.7	60	4.6
Irish potato	10.0	59	5.9
Maize	11.0	43	4.7
Rice	9.0	54	4.9
Millet	12.1	44	5.3
Wheat	13.4	44	5.9

Source: From P. Payne, "Protein deficiency or starvation?" *New Scientist* (the weekly review of science and technology), November 1974.

tant is that the proteins should contain reasonable levels of the essential amino acids lysine and tryptophan. Alexander (1975) describes the work of various breeders in using the rare maize endosperm mutant, opaque-2, which is high in both lysine and tryptophan, together with another high-quality mutant, floury-2. One difficulty in breeding for yield is that protein content is relatively reduced when higher yields are obtained, but hybrids having the opaque-2 gene contain so much highly nutritional protein that a lower yield is gladly accepted. In Ethiopia, researchers have found a high-lysine trait in barley, conditioned by a recessive allele *lys*. Attempts are also under way to breed for high protein in root and tuber crops as well. Cassava is notoriously low in protein, though potatoes possess levels not much inferior to those of the major cereals, and their proteins have a better amino-acid balance.

Oil- and fat-producing plants are also of importance and have been so since the very earliest times. Evidence of oil seeds such as olive, flax, poppy, and *Camelina* from Near Eastern archaeological sites (Renfrew, 1973) indicates their probable use for cooking or lighting. Radish and sesame were also used as a source of oil (Brothwell, 1969).

Nowadays there is a very wide range of plants used for oils and fats, including soybean, cottonseed, groundnut (peanut), maize, sunflower, rapeseed, safflower, sesame, olive, copra, and oil palm. On the whole, production has been increasing faster in developed countries than in the developing countries (see Table 5.2, from Röbbelen, 1975). According to Röbbelen, one of the breeder's main concerns is to select varieties with an ever-higher oil content in the harvested product; thus the proportion of oil-bearing to non-oil-bearing tissues in the seeds or fruits is of great importance. Quality is obviously of great value also (see Table 5.3).

Questions of vitamins and mineral content must not be overlooked, especially in fruits and vegetables, and appropriate substances must be bred for in stimulants, spices, and condiments.

Adaptation

Adaptation is an immensely complex subject. Not only does the crop plant need to be generally adapted to the soil and climate of a particular region; it can also be bred to tolerate a wide or a narrow range of conditions. Most of the newer wheats and rices are bred to

Table 5.2 Net exports of the principal vegetable oils and oil-producing seeds from primary producing countries (1,000 metric tons in oil equivalent).

Country	1960	1964	1968
Canada	164	162	217
Ceylon	74	155	77
West Malaysia	134	139	354
Nigeria	600	669	520
Argentina	285	230	244
Brazil	41	110	122
China	364	141	255
Congo	236	168	210
Indonesia	276	267	275
Phillipines	732	769	684
Rumania	43	42	135
Senegal	226	245	258
Soviet Union	111	202	852
Spain	137	105	43
Sudan	84	135	94
United States	1,426	1,952	1,946
Total	5,835	6,603	7,450
Developed Countries	1,008	2,366	2,393
Developing countries	3,445	3,782	3,640
Centrally planned economies	578	455	1,417

Source: After Röbbelen, 1975.

produce good yields where there is good soil moisture but cannot adapt themselves to low-moisture or near-drought conditions, when the yields drop catastrophically. On the other hand, the old land races, or primitive forms, as they are called, can withstand a lower moisture content without such a sharp drop in yield, even though normally, under optimal conditions, their yields are not as great as those of the highly bred varieties. This ability of the more primitive varieties to withstand poor growth conditions, owing to genes and gene complexes that have evolved for many thousands of years, is of great value. We have been in danger of discarding these old land races because of their poor yields. Luckily, they are now being preserved and are beginning to be used in new plant-breeding programs.

Resistance to drought is becoming of ever greater importance in the modern world, because as land with good soils and rainfall becomes used up and as still more is needed to grow food, marginal lands must be brought into production. In general, the dry zones of the world are found in developing countries that desperately need to raise food production, areas such as the northern African countries, those of the Sahel zone south of the Sahara, the Near East, Pakistan, and many parts of India. For these areas sorghum and millets and other drought-adapted crops are the candidates for the breeder's initial material.

The problem of drought resistance is of such importance that

Table 5.3   Oil extraction rates for oil-producing seeds.

Seed	Percentage of oil extracted
Babassu kernels	63
Castor seed	45
Copra	64
Cottonseed	16
Groundnuts, shelled	45
Groundnuts, unshelled	32
Hemp seed	24
Kapok seed	18
Linseed	34
Mustard seed	23
Niger seed	35
Oiticica seed	45
Olives	15
Palm kernels	47
Perilla seed	37
Poppy seed	41
Rapeseed	35
Safflower seed	30
Sesame seed	45
Shea nuts	45
Sunflower seed	35
Soybeans	17
Tung nuts	16
Others	30

Source: After Röbbelen, 1975.

two international institutes have recently been founded, supported by the World Bank through an organization known as the Consultative Group on International Agricultural Research (CGIAR). One of them, the International Crop Research Institute for the Semi-Arid Tropics (ICRISAT), is situated near Hyderabad in India and has special responsibilities for research, breeding, and conservation with sorghum, millets, chickpeas, groundnuts (peanuts), and pigeon peas. The second, the International Center for Agricultural Research in Dry Areas (ICARDA) has been established in Syria and Lebanon to take responsibility for research, breeding, and conservation with barley, lentils, broad beans (*Vicia faba*), wheat, and chickpeas.

Drought resistance must be distinguished from heat tolerance, since the two are not always associated with each other. Both are extremely complex and difficult to analyze. Dorofeev (1975), in evaluating wheat material for drought resistance, pointed out that the degree of resistance in a cereal variety was the result of the interaction of several morphological and physiological characters that enable the plant to tolerate low soil-moisture, high temperature, and low humidity over a long period of time. He found little drought resistance from the plants collected in the Vavilov centers of origin — which was rather surprising. In fact, after screening 19,000 accessions of spring and autumn wheat he found only 150 with good drought-resistance. These came mostly from Uzbekistan, Turkmenistan, Syria, Afghanistan, India, Chile, Mexico, and Canada. The inheritance mechanisms have not been well studied, though it is known that drought resistance is based on complex polygenic characters. Work on *Phaseolus* beans and millets, as well as other promising crops, is under way. Evaluation is generally undertaken in the field, because laboratory methods for analyzing drought resistance are not well formulated.

Resistance to cold is also of considerable importance as the attempts to expand the limits of cultivation push farming further north and to higher altitudes. Considerable success in such areas has been obtained with potatoes, and there is copious literature on the subject (Dearborn, 1969; Richardson and Estrada, 1971; Ross and Rowe, 1969). Frost resistance in potatoes seems to occur chiefly in the wild species such as *Solanum acaule, S. megistacrolobum*, and *S. demissum*. Where it is found in the cultivated species, such as *S. juzepczukii*, *S. curtilobum*, and *S. ajanhuri*, experimental taxonomic studies have shown that the resistance comes from hybridization with one of the wild frost-resisters. Breeders have used these species, either the wild or the cultivated ones or both, as starting material for several new varieties now on the market.

Cold tolerance is discussed also by Dorofeev (1975) for cereals, where a considerable amount of physiological work has been undertaken to elucidate the nature such of tolerance. Some 200 varieties of cereals have been demonstrated to show high frost-resistance in the Soviet Union, based on accessions obtained from the Soviet Union itself, Canada, and the United States. Innes (1975) describes the need for varieties of *Phaseolus vulgaris* to grow at the lower temperatures of an English summer, since in general the species is accustomed to much warmer growth temperatures, and accessions with promise have been obtained from Central and South America. This, then, is another important feature – not necessarily tolerance to frost but merely the ability to mature seeds under conditions cooler than those to which the crop is normally accustomed.

Salinity tolerance is yet another problem for breeders to contend with and is very much linked with the problem of drought tolerance, since drought and salinity are frequently found together. Salinity tolerance has been found in a wide range of species (see Udovenko, 1975) but it is highly complex, and based on the combined effects of many genetic factors. Salinity itself also differs, according to whether sodium, potassium, or other salts are present, and in what proportions. Irrigation projects in arid zones have often increased salinity by not providing adequate drainage for the irrigation water. Salt tolerance in wheat and in rice varieties can be found (Cooper, 1970; Ayers, Brown, and Wadleigh, 1952; Tahir and Hussain, 1975), but much more work is needed to select and breed from the best and most tolerant strains.

Disease resistance

Breeding crops for resistance to pests and pathogens has perhaps occupied more breeders' time and more space in the literature than any other breeding activity. Resistances to fungi, bacteria, viruses, viroids, insects, mites, and nematodes must be sought out by appropriate screening methods. Mangelsdorf (1965) points out that crops growing in pure stand over millions of acres provide vast culture media for invading fungi. The production of resistant varieties of the crop acts only as an efficient screening mechanism for sorting out new genetic combinations of the fungi with new sets of genes conferring different pathogenicity. Hence, as Mangelsdorf puts it, "The result is a permanent cold war between the plant breeders and the fungus pests which neither completely wins."

The relative merits of horizontal (nonspecific) and vertical (single-gene) resistance have been discussed at length (van der Plank, 1968). For more than 30 years, breeding to combat late blight (*Phytophthora infestans*) in potatoes was based on single hypersensitivity genes, and complex schemes were set out to explain the genetic systems of host and pathogen. However, every time a potato cultivar was bred for specific resistance to a pathotype or a series of pathotypes, other races of the pathotype would emerge that would kill the "resistant" host after a very short time. In the early 1950s it was felt that such vertical resistance breeding was never going to produce results of even short-term value. Accordingly, a gradual switch to generalized, nonspecific, or horizontal resistance was made. The horizontal resistance is polygenically controlled but was found in the same group of wild species as the vertical type of resistance. Although it did not provide complete immunity to any pathotype, the end results were far more effective. Even in Mexico, the apparent center of origin of the blight fungus, where every conceivable pathotype seems to be present, horizontal resistance has continued to stand the test of time, while selections showing only vertical resistance are killed off within a few weeks.

The development of breeding for horizontal resistance is now being used to protect wheat against stripe rust races with apparently very promising results (see CIMMYT Today, 1977). In most programs of this sort, a combination of the genes responsible for both vertical and horizontal resistance is generally built into the crop plant varieties. Breeding programs for resistance to viruses, bacteria, insects, and nematodes follow similar patterns, although many of these programs are at the stage of vertical resistance in a plant; in fact, however, this seems to hold up well against certain pathogens such as nematodes.

An interesting example of bacterial resistance breeding can be seen in the potato, which in general is completely susceptible to bacterial wilt (*Pseudomonas solanacearum*). The world collection of potatoes was screened for wilt resistance to no avail until six lines of a primitive diploid cultivated species, *Solanum phureja*, from Colombia were found to exhibit a high degree of resistance (Thurston and Lozano, 1968). Resistance is based on a number of dominant genes, plus modifiers (Rowe and Sequeira, 1970) and can be transferred to *S. tuberosum* without difficulty. This was the beginning of an effort in the warmer regions of the world to breed potatoes for resistance to this disease. It should be noted that only a few clones from one part of the total distribution area of *S. phureja* showed resistance.

Potato breeding for resistance to nematodes has followed a similar pattern, in that the resistance genes to the potato cyst nematodes are localized to Peru, Bolivia, and northwestern Argentina. Resistance to various pathotypes is found in a number of different wild species and in the cultivated tetraploid, subsp. *andigena*, which is the original of the two tetraploid subspecies of *S. tuberosum*. Evidence is building up that this resistance has penetrated into the cultigen from a wild resistant tetraploid, *S. oplocense* (Astley and Hawkes, 1979). The F_1 hybrid of this cross, which has been named *S sucrense*, is a well-known weed species in central Bolivia.

Resistance to the insect transmitted viruses of potatoes is also limited to the warmer and drier areas of north-central Mexico and northwestern Argentina, where no doubt the insect vectors are frequent. Resistance to the insects themselves also occurs in those regions. This would seem to indicate a clear cause-and-effect mechanism of resistance to insects and to the viruses that some of them transmit, in the same areas through the selection pressures involved (Hawkes, 1958). Qualset (1975) describes a similar case of resistance to the barley yellow dwarf virus localized in Ethiopia, and Chang and others (1975) mention various localized genetic resistances to rise diseases and pests in Southeast Asia.

The conclusions of this section are abundantly clear. Genetic characters for yield, quality, high nutritional levels, adaptation and disease resistance are found sometimes in a wide range of breeding material, sometimes in a very narrow one. The problems are highly diverse, time consuming and almost always far more difficult and frustrating to solve than appears at first sight. Close collaboration is required between the breeder, on the one hand, and the phytopathologist, virologist, entomologist, or nematologist on the other.

The Loss of Diversity

In advanced countries such as the United States, Canada, and the countries in Europe and elsewhere, our crops tend to be extremely uniform. Much of their original genetic diversity has been lost, and the crops are described as possessing a "narrow genetic base." Although uniformity of yield, quality, growth characteristics and maturity are all necessary for the highly sophisticated farming technology that we apply to our crops, this uniformity also holds a hidden danger: it can offer an open doorway to attacks by pest and pathogen. With a uniform crop variety, or a range of rather similar varieties, once a strain of a pathogen becomes adapted to attack it, the whole crop can be lost in a very short time.

A narrow genetic base of crops can be highly dangerous for the future. To take examples from the United States (National Academy of Sciences, 1972), of 14 major crops in that country (Table 5.4), including wheat, maize, potatoes, peanuts, and soybean, 9 crops (64%) have 4 or fewer major varieties, which dominate some 60–70% of crop acreage. Indeed, with millet, peanut, and peas, over 90% of each crop is dominated by a very few varieties (Table 5.4).

This vulnerability of crops in the United States became extremely clear in 1970 with the advent of the Southern corn blight (*Helminthosporium maydis*). A single source of cytoplasm had been used in developing the majority of the Corn Belt hybrids, and this cytoplasm conveyed corn-blight susceptibility to all the varieties that contained it. The lesson was clear: great genetic uniformity, while excellent for short-term farming and marketing needs, has its very real dangers. Uniformity, when disease susceptibility is concerned, may rest on a single gene or a single kind of cytoplasm, or a few genes only. Indeed, for a major epidemic to take place, the crop needs to be uniform for only *one* character, providing that this character confers susceptibility to a pathotype (race) of a particular pest or disease. These examples clearly point to the fact that genetic diversity in our crops is extremely necessary. This could be combined within a single variety or in a group of varieties of the

Table 5.4 Acreage and farm value of major United States crops and the extent to which a few varieties dominate that acreage (1969 figures).

Crop	Acreage (millions)	Value (millions of dollars)	Total number of varieties	Number of major varieties	Acreage (percent)
Bean, dry	1.40	143	25	2	60
Bean, snap	0.30	99	70	3	76
Cotton	11.20	1,200	50	3	53
Corn[a]	66.30	5,200	197[b]	6	71
Millet	2.00	−	−	3	100
Peanut	1.40	312	15	9	95
Peas	0.40	80	50	2	96
Potato	1.40	616	82	4	72
Rice	1.80	449	14	4	65
Sorghum	16.80	795	?	?	?
Soybean	42.40	2,500	62	6	56
Sugar beet	1.40	367	16	2	42
Sweet potato	0.13	63	48	1	69
Wheat	44.30	1,800	269	9	50

Source: National Academy of Sciences, 1972.
a. Corn includes seeds, forage, and silage.
b. Released public inbreds only.

crop, or even in breeding lines that are kept ready to introduce as new varieties when the need arises.

On the whole, legislation in the United States, the European Economic Community, and probably elsewhere, is strongly opposed to crop diversity. Thus, Hutchinson (in Hawkes, 1978, chapter 19) states that "in the European Economic Community we are engaged in making sure that none but the most advanced varieties are allowed to be sold in the area, thereby very greatly restricting the diversity that is available to us." A law prohibiting the raising of more than one variety of cotton in the San Joachim Valley of California is also a potentially very dangerous situation.

At this point we should distinguish between diversity existing within individual varieties and general genetic diversity available to breeders. Hutchinson (1978) has argued that it might be better for crop varieties to be less pure, and more diverse, so as to resist pathogen attacks. Wheat breeders creating "multiline" varieties are doing just that, but legislation in general demands a high level of purity in seeds offered for sale. This is the complete opposite of the situation 50 to 100 years ago when farmers grew what are termed "land races," which could not even be called varieties and were highly diverse populations and mixtures of genotypes.

The other kind of diversity is that existing in a very wide range of genetically different varieties (cultivars) which are still offered by the seedsmen and can form the basis of new plant breeding programs. If this diversity is still to be found, the genetic base may be broad enough, but under modern farming and farming legislation in the advanced countries it is rapidly disappearing, as the examples already quoted have shown.

Breeders' Needs for Diversity

It is clear that the more genetic diversity that can be available to the breeder, the wider range of choice he will have in selecting the appropriate kinds of diversity for his breeding programs, although for any one crop, the breeder may not need or use more than a very small amount of what is available. In the latter part of the nineteenth century and the early decades of the twentieth century, breeders were content to go not much further for their material than the old land races and varieties that were then available in their own countries or from neighboring ones. In the last 50 years or so, however, a much wider range of genetic diversity is required.

Genetic Resources

It is customary nowadays to use the phrase "genetic resources" to define the total genetic diversity of cultivated species and their wild relatives, much of which may be valuable to breeders. The types of material are generally distinguished as follows:

1. *Currently grown commercial varieties* (cultivars) from the breeder's own country or exotic ones introduced from other countries.

2. *Obsolete commercial varieties* that are now no longer commercially grown but which may still be obtained from seed merchants or individual collections.
3. *Breeding lines and stocks*, which may be the breeder's own stocks or those obtained from other breeders, not yet developed into commercial varieties but possessing some potential value.
4. *Induced or natural mutations* occurring within the breeder's own collections, obtainable by exchange or developed by other scientists.
5. *Old land races* obtained from remote areas or small garden plots where the new, highly bred cultivars have not been introduced. These are races or populations that have not been bred as varieties but that, under natural and artificial selection (probably largely of an unconscious nature), have become adapted to the conditions under which they are cultivated.
6. *Primitive forms* of crop plants collected from the old Vavilovian centers of origin and diversity. They are highly diverse genetically, often having been grown as mixtures of species as well as diverse populations of one species. Some authors do not distinguish these from land races.
7. *Weed races* occurring as part of the crop-weed complexes in gene centers. In many instances they incorporate useful genes derived from wild prototypes or related wild species which have moved from the weedy forms into the crops themselves. In these instances nature has helped the breeder by inserting genes (some of them useful) from wild species into a suitable "cultivated" genetic background.
8. *Related wild species* that occur sometimes in the gene centers of cultivated plants, sometimes far outside them, and that can be crossed with the cultigens.

All these materials can be thought of as genetic resources, since they are all part of the gene pool of the cultigen or of related wild species. Often, however, the term *genetic resources* refers more specifically to types 5, 6, 7, and 8.

Sources of Diversity

It has been customary of late to claim that all major advances in plant breeding have come or will come in the future from plant materials in the Vavilovian gene centers. This overstates the case. In three of our major crops — cotton, wheat, and rice — the great advances have come from the exploitation of diversity *within the advanced cultivars* (Hutchinson, in Hawkes 1978, p. 256). Resistance to bacterial blight in cotton, for example, came from West Africa, which cannot be considered one of the centers of origin or diversity of cotton in the Vavilovian sense.

The Norin semi-dwarf wheats and the dwarf rice varieties that have contributed to the success of the Green Revolution came from advanced cultivars in China and Japan. However, these dwarf strains of wheat and rice were clearly bred from old land races or primitive forms in the ancient Chinese centers of origin and diversity. Thus these last two examples do not completely disagree with the statement that much useful genetic diversity occurs in the gene centers. In some instances, as for late blight resistance in potatoes mentioned above, the resistance genes are to be found in wild species in Mexico where the fungus seems to have evolved, and not among the primitive forms of cultivated potato in the South American gene center.

Notwithstanding these examples, there is indeed much evidence of useful genetic characters to be found in primary or secondary gene centers.

A good example of this is resistance to coffee rust, *Hemileia vastatrix*. It arrived in South and Central America in 1970, and some 30 physiological races or pathotypes are known. Some resistance genes have been identified in the cultivated *Coffea arabica* coffee, and also in the wild coffee species *C. liberica* and *C. canephora*. Genes for both vertical and horizontal resistance to the rust races are being used frequently in breeding, both from the distribution areas of the wild species in West Africa and the center of origin for cultivated coffee in Ethiopia.

Diseases of rice offer another interesting example of localization of resistance genes. Resistance to bacterial leaf streak has been found in *"spontanea"* varieties of *Oryza sativa*, the Asian cultivated rice, and in the related wild rice species *O. rufipogon*, in Southeast Asia. *O. rufipogon* is the basic species from which *O. nivara* and *O. sativa* are though to have been derived, while *"spontanea"* rices are considered to be crosses between *O. nivara* and *O. sativa*, (Ng et al., 1982). All three species are thought to have originated in Southeast

Asia, one of the important crop gene centers designated by Vavilov. In addition, resistance to grassy stunt virus is found only in *O. nivara*, again in the Southeast Asian center. However, resistance to other rice diseases, such as blast disease, is very scattered, being found in Thailand, Vietnam, China, Burma, Sri Lanka, India, and Africa (Chang et al., 1975).

Resistance to *Avena* (oat) diseases is sometimes to be found in wild species as with crown rust resistance, in *A. sterilis* and *A. barbata*, but much rust resistance is found within breeding collections.

From these few examples we can see clearly that useful characters can be found sometimes within the gene centers and sometimes outside them, often in the cultigens and quite frequently in related wild species. In the past, success has been obtained by breeding from advanced cultivars, but as new and more rigorous requirements present themselves, breeders are more and more turning to primitive forms, weed races, and related wild species for the characters desired. We see also that some desired resistance characters seem to be scattered throughout the distribution area of a species (as for blast disease of rice and wart disease and virus X disease of potatoes); others are clearly localized (as for yellow dwarf disease in barley, and grassy stunt virus in rice).

Plant Breeding Materials

From the foregoing section I have given examples from various types of material, both wild and cultivated. Much has been said in favor of using wild species as initial material in the search for adaptation and resistance characters. However, this is because there is often no resistance to be found in the cultigen itself, so that the breeder must go where he can for the qualities he needs. The sequence of searching for initial material is generally as follows:

1. Screen (evaluate) working and other collections, national breeding stocks, breeding lines, mutants, and current and obsolete national and exotic cultivars.
2. Screen the world collections or gene banks for land races and the primitive cultivars from the gene centers and elsewhere.
3. If the required characters are not found in these, the breeder

should screen wild-species collections, not only of those species that are assumed to be the wild prototypes but also weed species and other plant materials known to be more or less related to the cultigen.
4. Very occasionally, intergeneric hybrids may be attemped, as, for instance, with the well-known cross between *Triticum* (wheat) and *Secale* (rye), known to breeders as *Triticale*.

The choices are usually made in this order, starting with the national or working collections because those are nearer at hand and therefore easiest to use; it is rather doubtful, however, whether the desired characters would generally be found in them, since the material should be well known already and will most probably be part of the same gene pool from which the existing cultivars have been taken. Because of this, for many crops, such as for potatoes until the 1930s, the genetic base available to breeders has been dangerously narrow. Since national and international collections have become much more varied than they were some 20 or 30 years ago, the base has now broadened considerably.

There are some good reasons for not using wild species in a breeding program and other good reasons for using them (Hawkes, 1977a; Harlan, 1976).

Against the use of wild species is the fact that they may be more difficult to cross, and the hybrids, when formed, may be wholly or partly sterile. Wild species may be of a different ploidy level than the cultivars, and their relationships to the cultigens may not be well known. Most important of all, the genetic background of wild species, by definition, is a wild one, so that most features, apart from the single desired one, will be highly undesirable. They will contribute poor yield and probably poor quality and unfavorable agronomic characters in general. Furthermore, if they are not closely allied to the cultigen, their modifier complexes, which alter the effects of other genes, may be very distinct. Long and tedious back-crossing programs and the breakage of undesirable linkages may also be needed before something like a reasonable breeding line can be produced.

A whole program of "pre-breeding," or "parental-line breeding," as it is called, may need to be carried out before the practical breeder has the "wild" characters in the right kind of "cultivated" background. Naturally, if the wild material is gathered from the crop-weed complexes, so much introgression from one to the other will already have taken place that the problem of transference of genes from weed to crop will not be very difficult (Astley and Hawkes, 1979). On the other hand, in such cases it is fairly certain that the transference will have already taken place without the help of the breeder. For example, frost resistance from the wild potato species *Solanum acaule* has already moved into the cultigen through the hybrids *S. juzepczukii* and *S. curtilobum*, as I have mentioned previously. There is evidence also that this frost resistance, as well as virus resistance, has been chaneled right through into the tetraploid *andigena* cultivars.

In another publication (Hawkes, 1977a) I have described the various difficulties encountered by the breeder in the transference of desirable qualities from wild species to cultigens and have distinguished about five levels of complexity in this process, progressing from easy to very difficult:

1. *Wild species and cultigen belonging to the same gene pool.* Examples of this with potatoes have just been given.
2. *Wild and cultivated species belonging to separate gene pools*, but fertility of the hybrids is very high, and regular bivalent pairing is normal. For instance, Chang and others (1975) point out that the only source of resistance to grassy stunt virus in rice is to be found in the wild species *Oryza nivara*, which is at the same ploidy level as *O. sativa* and can be crossed with it quite easily.
3. *Wild and cultivated species having a different number of chromosomes*, often with a different genome formula, but where fertility can be restored if necessary by amphidiploidy, that is, chromosome doubling of the hybrid. An interesting example is described by Julen and Ellerström (1973), who crossed a wild type of kale (*Brassica oleracea*) with cultivated turnip rape (*B. rapa*). After chromosome doubling, new oil rape (*B. napus*) types were obtained having a higher degree of winter hardiness than was previously known. This is an excellent example of the production of new types of variation based on a model already provided by nature (see also Muntzing, 1966).
4. *Crosses requiring special techniques.* An example of this may be found in *Lycopersicon* (see Rick, 1967), where the cross between

the cultivated tomato *Lycopersicon esculentum* and a wild species, *L. peruvianum*, could be made only through the use of embryo culture to enable the F_1 hybrids to survive the early embryonic stages. Another example from potatoes was given by Dionne (1961, 1963), who successfully obtained the almost impossible cross of *S. acaule* × *S. bulbocastanum*, in order to transfer late-blight resistance from the latter species to *S. tuberosum*.

5. *Very wide hybridizations*. Although *Triticale* is a wide intergeneric cross of *Triticum* (wheat) and *Secale* (rye), the cross is accomplished quite easily and has been encountered several times in nature. In general, wide crosses, that is, between rather unrelated species, are very difficult to make and require some special technique, such as *in vitro* fertilization or protoplast fusion.

There is no time here to deal with protoplast fusion, but suffice it to say that we are on the brink of exciting new developments. Quite a large number of protoplast fusions have been effected, but very few have been brought forward to the whole-plant stage with the genomes of both parents relatively intact. We must still wait for the results from these methods, which will probably not be long in arriving.

Having discussed some aspects of the value of the diversity of crop plants to the breeder, some failures and many successes are apparent. Perhaps we shall accomplish more in the future, but for the present I can do no better than agree with Hutchinson (1965) by stressing that we need to study the physiology of our crops more and more, as an aid to breeding and utilization of as wide a range of the existing genetic resources as possible. For the present, perhaps "our limitations are the limitations of our scientific insight and imagination, rather than of the biological material with which we work" (Hutchinson, 1965).

6

The Exploration and Storage of Crop
Plant Diversity

⌈Without a wide range of variability in crop plants, the plant breeder cannot hope to solve problems of increased yield, higher nutritive quality, a better range of adaptation, and better disease resistance. The needs are clear, since population pressures and the demands in rich and poor countries alike for a decent standard of living are calling for greater food production. Rather than extend farming into areas where it is more difficult to obtain a good yield because of soil and climate limitations, and rather than destroy the last remains of tropical rain forest and mountain vegetation, we must try to produce better crop yields for a given amount of cultivated land. In the developed countries, farming can at times be too efficient, resulting in embarrassing surpluses that are not sensibly dealt with. However, the situation is very different in developing countries.⌋

In fact, in the world in general we need better varieties of crops from the plant breeders, which can be produced only if a wide genetic base of crop plant diversity is available, as I have discussed in the previous chapter.

I have shown how this diversity has evolved and where it can be found in a more concentrated form, in Vavilov's centers of diversity. I have also touched on the value now being placed on wild species related to our cultigens, in providing characters of importance, especially in respect to resistance to pests and pathogens, and in extending the adaptive range of a crop plant.

If the problem were no greater than one of gathering the genetic material whenever it was needed, there would be very few difficulties other than those, by no means minor ones, of breeding varieties that would incorporate the desired features. Unfortunately, this is not the case, since a marked reduction in genetic diversity, or genetic erosion, as it is often called, has been taking place with increasing intensity in the last four or five decades.

Genetic Erosion

By the early 1950s, concern was being expressed that the genetic variation of cultivated plants in their centers of diversity was beginning to disappear. Such genetic erosion was not confined to one crop or to one region but was widespread, even though it was more intense in certain areas than in others. The apparently inexhaustible gene pools of Vavilov's day were beginning to dry up. A number of authors have drawn attention to genetic erosion and the genetic vulnerability of our major and minor crops in different parts of the world (National Academy of Sciences, 1972; Harlan, 1972, 1975; Frankel, 1970a, 1970b, 1972, 1974; Hawkes, 1971). All express concern for our diminishing genetic heritage and urge action towards its conservation (see Fig. 6.1).

The situation is now frighteningly clear. Genetic erosion has been taking place partly, though not entirely, as a result of the plant breeders' successful activities in breeding better varieties, which have been gradually replacing the older populations of primitive forms and land races in the regions where diversity had been greatest. These new, highly bred varieties are being adopted by farmers because of their greater yields or resistance to disease, and thus the highly diverse ancient land-races are gradually dropping out of cultivation. Cultivated plants depend completely on man, and if, for one season only, we do not sow a variety, it will disappear forever.

What has been taking place, therefore, is a destruction of the genetic richness of the older populations of cultivated species and their replacement by a limited number of standard varieties. This is the paradox, since the breeder, who means well, is destroying by his actions the genetic base for a new generation of varieties. Further-

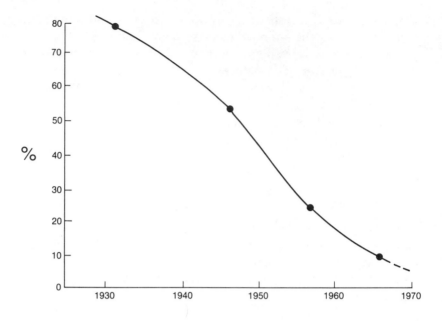

Fig. 6.1   Proportion of the Greek wheat crop contributed by old, indigenous cultivars between 1930 and 1966. (Bennett, 1971.)

more, more-advanced farming practices are removing the attendant weed races and tidying up the fields and roadsides so that even the related wild species are suffering erosion of their former genetic variability.

Much praise and some criticism has been given to the Green Revolution, in which new, high-yielding, short-strawed varieties of wheat and rice have been bred and introduced into Third World countries. At their best, they have helped solve many food problems. At their worst, they have caused a catastrophic genetic erosion, especially in Turkey, Iraq, Afghanistan, Pakistan, and India (Fig. 6.2). In those countries it is now quite difficult to find the older bread-wheat varieties, even though they were still common some 20 years ago (Frankel, 1973). The reports of recent expeditions to Pakistan (Bennett, in Frankel, 1973; Witcombe, 1975; Lamberts, 1977, personal communication) have drawn attention to the fact that all the regions of easy access near the main roads and paths

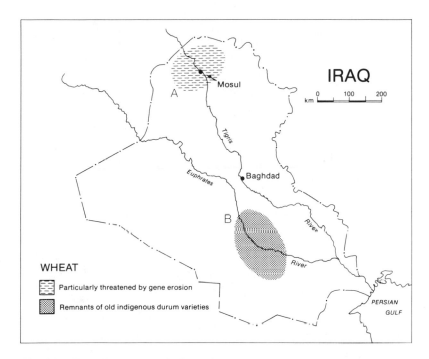

Fig. 6.2 Genetic erosion of wheat diversity in Iraq. (Frankel, 1973, based on data provided by Kuckuck.)

were planted with new, highly bred varieties (Fig. 6.3). Far away, in the areas remote from easy communications with the cities and towns, genetic diversity could still be found and collected, but this situation will not last long, and scientists are engaging more and more in rescue operations, before the last remnants of what must now often be called the "former centers of diversity" disappear from the farms forever.

The Food and Agriculture Organization of the United Nations (FAO), together with the International Board for Plant Genetic Resources (IBPGR), has taken action on this matter of genetic erosion and is spreading the awareness of the emergency that is developing in certain parts of the world. Not only annual field crops but even longer-lived perennials such as bush, fruit, and timber trees are also threatened. Wild species related to the crops are threatened by the destruction of their natural habitats. Those that are unrelated but that may still be needed for the future must

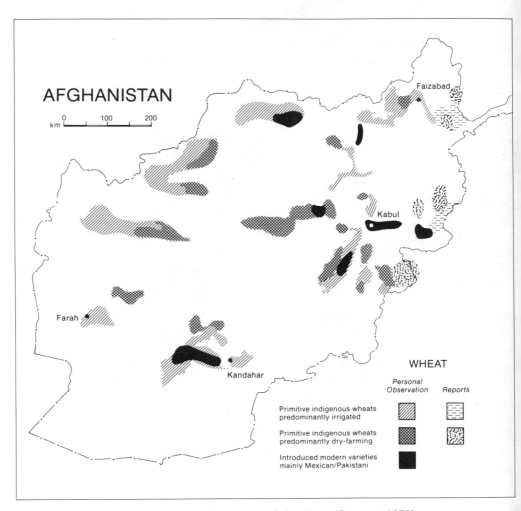

Fig. 6.3 Genetic erosion of wheat diversity in Afghanistan. (Bennett, 1973).

also be conserved in some way, perhaps in biosphere reserves, for instance (Hegnauer, 1975).

Thus the preservation of diversity, both in natural reserves and in special germplasm collections, or gene banks, as they have been called, is an essential activity for conserving our genetic heritage. Even though we are not quite certain as to what we shall need in the future, we know what is necessary today and can at least extrapolate our needs by means of intelligent guesses. We can thus set out a list of urgent tasks to help us conserve germplasm.

1. We need to evaluate the situation to understand what is available in the field or in collections, what is most under threat, and how it should be further explored and collected.
2. We need to decide on the priorities and strategies for storage, whether in natural reserves, in living collections (orchards, arboreta, botanical gardens, and experimental stations), or in seed, pollen, or tissue-culture banks.
3. We must make sure that the material is available for use and that it is undergoing screening or evaluation, so that its potential value to breeders is made clear.
4. There must be some way to store and retrieve information by computer systems that can transmit to breeders data on the useful qualities of the materials and on the gene banks in which they are to be found.
5. Scientists must be trained to undertake these tasks, expecially those scientists from developing countries where the major part of our genetic resources still exists.
6. Finally, there must be a well-organized world system to coordinate activities, to prevent duplication of effort, and, even more important, to provide scientific and administrative initiatives.

Exploration and Collection of Genetic Resources

Aspects of exploration, evaluation, and conservation of genetic resources were dealt with by Frankel and Bennett (1970), by Frankel and Hawkes (1975), and by Matsuo (1975) in various edited works, with different authors dealing with various aspects of the subject. A general field manual for collecting genetic resources was published by Hawkes (1980). Most of us agree that exploration and collection of genetic resources needs to be undertaken, but a careful assessment of the problem must first be made.

Surveys

At three planning conferences on this topic for potatoes, arranged by the International Potato Center in Peru (CIP) (1973, 1976, 1979), guidelines were established for exploration based on (1) threats of genetic erosion, (2) plant breeders' needs, and (3) taxonomic or other interests and the lack of living material. Priorities were assessed country by country and group by group, in descending order from *E* (emergency), *A* (high priority), *B* (medium priority), to *C* (low priority). This classification has served well and has enabled CIP scientists and others to fulfill a five year collecting plan in about three years.

Other crops are now being dealt with in the same way as potatoes, through crop committees established by the IBPGR. In addition, a valuable survey of crop genetic resources was organized by Frankel, and a publication on the results was edited by him in 1973. The individual crops were surveyed by experts through correspondence or in the field, and the survey covers the major cereals, grain legumes, tuber crops, coffee, cacao, condiments, and tree fruits. Maps show species distribution or the localities where collections have been made, and the text draws attention to areas where the plants are being threatened.

Such information is of great value in showing planners which areas need urgent or emergency treatment and thus helps in establishing priorities. Both funds and trained personnel are scarce, however, so that it is impossible to attend to all crops and areas simultaneously. In all such surveys, and indeed in expedition work also, a thorough knowledge of the taxonomic and agronomic features of the crop is essential, as is a good grounding in the taxonomy of the related wild species. Knowledge of evolutionary relationships, cytology, and crossability of the wild and cultivated forms is also highly desirable.

The need to include weedy forms and wild species in such surveys is clear. Such forms may not always be under threat but may, on the other hand, be urgently needed by breeders to provide useful characters not found in the cultivated species. The existence of such characters may be investigated or may be definitely known, though additional resistance to a wide range of disease pathotypes is still often sought. Sometimes from a purely taxonomic viewpoint it will be desirable to collect material of other wild species not so far studied in the living state, or whose relationship to the cultigen is uncertain. Biosystematic studies of such wild relatives (or suspected relatives) can help to make more material available to the breeders. This again stresses the essential need for biosystematic studies on the wild relatives of cultivated plants, as an aid in plant breeding.

Exploration and collection

For most purposes, the meanings of *exploration* and *collection* largely overlap, because when a scientist explores the occurrence and distribution of a crop, he or she makes collections, too. At times, however, living collections cannot be taken if seeds or fruits have not reached the right stage for harvesting. Under these circumstances, arrangements must be made with local personnel to make the collections later.

The objectives and methods of the genetic resources collector are very distinct from those of the botanical collector, a point generally not well understood by either the taxonomist or the plant breeder. It is essential to give some practical training to the genetic resources collector, who must be encouraged to sample populations, rather than merely collect individuals, and to take adequate amounts of material in each sample. The underlying theories of population genetics do not need to be understood thoroughly before one can become a collector. Nevertheless, a study of population structure is needed in order to work out optimum sampling strategies (Jain, 1975, Bradshaw, 1975; Marshall and Brown, 1975). Since there are definite limits to the numbers of samples that can be collected and handled effectively, the keynote must be to try to capture a maximum amount of genetic diversity for a minimum number of samples.

Multiple sampling should be made throughout the total distribution area of the species, since the variability will certainly not be uniform in all parts, as I discussed in previous chapters. Certain genetic characters can be seen in very localized parts of the distribution areas of a species, such as the resistance to bacterial wilt (*Pseudomonas solanacearum*) found in one small area of *Sola-*

num phureja variation, and the resistance to yellow dwarf barley virus in Ethiopia (see Chapter 5). This localization has been discussed by Allard (1970a) who clearly distinguished between geographical variability, to which we have just been referring, and variability between and within populations. He points out that resistance to some diseases can be found throughout the whole range of a species, even though resistance to others can be localized. Variability in quantitative characters can also be localized, though this is more difficult to see at a glance.

Clinal patterns can be observed in wild species and therefore probably occur in crops also, though this has not been very well studied. Patchwork or mosaic variation between populations also occurs, sometimes within very short distances, even in outcrossing species, and this can also be seen in crops (Bradshaw, 1975). However, as Bradshaw points out, the situation has not been looked at in sufficient detail to give a clear genetical picture for any crop that is still in a primitive, unimproved state.

Sampling techniques

Marshall and Brown (1975) have given a clear indication of an optimum strategy for sampling. Defining as their aim the capture, with 95% certainty, of at least one copy of each variant having a frequency in the population greater than 5%, they advocate that a bulk sample of 50 seeds each from about 50 to 100 plants should be taken as a unit collection from each site (normally a single field) and that these plants should be chosen in a completely random manner. Bennett (1970) advocated starting at a randomly selected point and making a number of transects through the crop, sampling a spike or seed head every two or three paces. She advised taking as many as 200–500 spikes per sample, but Marshall and Brown have calculated that 50, or at most 100, are all that are required to complete a suitable population sample.

Although Marshall and Brown advocate strictly random sampling only, Bennett would play more safely by adding to each sample a biased sample if rare morphotypes of low frequency are seen in the crop. Completely biased sampling, whereby selections are made visually and not at random, is unacceptable, because we cannot tell at a glance what useful characters of growth, adaptation, or disease resistance are likely to be present, merely on visual inspection (see also Dinoor, 1975).

It is normally thought advisable to take a batch of clustered samplings from several fields in and around a village site, if cultivated plants are under survey, or from a small area of about one square kilometer if wild plants are being collected. This will capture the mosaic of interpopulation variation in a "target area." How, then, should we sample a complete region? Allard (1970a) advocates fewer samples in a climatically, altitudinally, and edaphically uniform region and many more where the environment appears to be highly variable. Bennett (1970) and Jain (1975) advocate a coarse-grid survey during the first collecting season, with subsequent rounds of sampling on a finer scale in areas later found to be of particular interest. This is a council of perfection, since if a region can be visited only once, or if the rate of genetic erosion is extremely rapid, then a thorough sampling of as many sites as possible, covering as broad a range of environments as possible, should be aimed at during a single visit before everything disappears.

Harlan (1975b) points out that variation in crops is often closely associated with ethnic groups, altitude, climate, and soil. Although agreeing with Marshall and Brown, he pleads for highly subjective and biased samples rather than random ones. Probably the best answer to this is a compromise, combining both random and nonrandom sampling in the way suggested by Bennett.

One of the problems that arises on a collecting trip is that it is not always possible to be in a field just before harvest when all the seeds are ripe. In many primitive regions, even the ripening times may not be uniform, since some peoples have a custom of selective hand-harvesting. If material is in the rick or stack, Bennett describes a way to take spikes out at random; if the grains or seeds have been threshed and are in bins or stores, several handfuls taken at random may suffice.

The sampling of root and tuber crops brings its own problems and has not received the attention from the population geneticists that it deserves. I have pointed out (1975) that with a crop such as potatoes, it is highly unlikely that populations, as such, can be found, even under truly primitive agricultural conditions. Strong artificial selection has reduced any semblance of a natural population to specially selected clones that can be recognized by eye. Thus a sample of each variant or morphotype can be collected without difficulty, since no village or market region will normally contain more than 50–200 morphotype samples.

One could ask whether this totally biased sampling is wrong, in that it will not allow other types of variation (physiological, disease resistance, and so on) to be sampled. However, we know from experience that the farmers are accustomed to relate the well-known morphotypes to physiological characters such as adaptation, palatability, cooking quality, and disease resistance. Therefore, all we can do is to collect one sample of each morphotype per village and market area, because the selection and elimination of types having less-desirable characters has already been accomplished by the farmers themselves. And since most vegetatively propagated crops outcross and are highly heterozygous, we know that each plant holds an enormous reservoir of genetic variation within it that is released when true seed is produced.

The sampling of wild species of vegetatively propagating plants is another matter, in that these species still occur as a series of populations. Problems arise with yams and other large-tubered crops over the sheer logistics of collecting and transporting bulky material from the field to the gene bank. Luckily, most of these wild species are still sexually fertile, and they can therefore be treated as seed crops. Where they are not (as in *Curcuma*), the population structure is probably much similar to that of the cultigens, and sampling can be effected as mentioned above.

Fruit-tree sampling has been discussed by Sykes (1975), Hawkes (1977b), and others. Sampling is easier in temperate regions, since populations can be identified more easily. In the tropics the populations are so diffuse that some doubts as to whether they are populations at all arises, where densities of 13–24 individuals per 100 hectares are considered normal (Whitmore, 1975).

Field documentation

Adequate field records are of great importance for genetic-resources sampling, as for normal botanical collecting. One must be wary of setting up an over-elaborate field-data sheet, because that would result in the collector's spending too much time filling out forms, to the detriment of his actual plant collections (see, for instance, Konzak, in Hawkes and Lange, 1973, pp. 28–36). It is probably unwise to ask for a great deal of information on topography, slope, stoniness, soil features, pH, and so forth, since experience indicates that plants adapted to one kind of habitat sometimes are found in a quite different one by chance. A basic or minimum data sheet could therefore include the following information (see Fig. 6.4):

1. Name of collector and collecting number.
2. Latin name of species (or at least of the genus or family).
3. Vernacular name.
4. Provenance, for example, country, province, district, nearest town or village, and distance and approximate direction from it (for example, 10 kilometers from a certain town in a southeasterly direction on trail or road to another town, by a certain river, or on a mountain range).
5. Latitude and longitude (to be filled in later from a map).
6. Date of collection.
7. Altitude of collection.
8. Photo number.
9. Type of material collected — seeds, tubers, cuttings, plants, herbarium, and so forth. The need for a voucher herbarium specimen wherever possible should be stressed.
10. Status — wild, weed, cultivated, escaped, and so forth.
11. Frequency — a rough estimate, such as abundant, frequent, occasional, or rare, is probably all that is required.
12. Habitat, set out in simple terms such as hedgerow, swamp forest, savannah, and so forth.
13. Special descriptive features that cannot be preserved in the herbarium specimens or seeds collected, such as the height of a tree, the type of branching, color, size, and shape of fruits, flower color and shape, leaf and stem color, leaf shape, if too large to fit onto a standard herbarium sheet. The features should be noted, but not the details that can be seen in the specimens collected.
14. Any other features of interest — for example, medicinal or economic properties, supposed resistance to disease, drought, cold, and so on.

All of this information can be coded for computer storage and can then be made available to breeders who wish to obtain more plant material from a particular area or to study the correlation between the distribution of some gene or adaptive complex in relation

Fig. 6.4 Minimum data sheet for genetic resources collections: (*left*) obverse side: Essential data; (*right*) reverse side: Optional data.

Expedition/Organization: ....

Country: ....

Team/Collector(s): .... *Collector's Number:* ....

Date of Collection: .... *Photo Number(s):* ....

Species Name: ....

Vernacular/Cultivar Name: ....

Locality: ....

....

....

Latitude: .... ° .... ′   *Longitude:* .... ° .... ′   *Altitude:* ....

Material: Seeds   Inflorescences   Roots/tubers   Live Plants   Herbarium

Sample: Population   Pure Line   Individual   Random   Non-Random

Status: Cultivated   Weed   Wild

Source: Field   Farm Store   Market   Shop   Garden   Wild vegetation

Original Source of Sample: ....

....

Frequency: Abundant   Frequent   Occasional   Rare

Habitat: ....

....

Descriptive Notes: ....

....

....

....

Collector   *Collector*   *Collector*   *Collector*

No: *No:*   *No:*   *No:*

Uses: ....
....

Cultural Practices: **Irrigated**   **Dry**

Season: .. *Approximate sowing dates:*..

               Approximate harvesting dates:...

Soil Observations: *Texture:* ....

                 Stoniness: ....

                 Depth: ....

                 Drainage: ....

                 Colour:...

Soil pH: ....

Land Form: *Aspect:* ....

              Slope:...

Topography: Swamp   Flood Plain   Level   Undulating

              Hilly   Hilly Dissected   Steeply Dissected

              Mountainous   Other (specify)

Plant Community: ....
....

Other Crops grown near or in rotation: ....
....

Pests/Pathogens: ....

Name and Address of Farmer: ....
....

Taxonomic Identification: ....

by..   *Date:* ....

Name of Institution: ....*Accession No.*......................

to some other series of parameters. Special field-data sheets for certain crops have frequently been designed, as one for crucifers shown in Figure 6.5.

The Conservation and Storage of Genetic Resources

The next problem is how to store the material collected. This is a matter of a totally different level of complexity than the problem of growing plants or storing seeds in botanical gardens, where it is not generally regarded as practicable to store more than one or a very few samples of each species. For genetic resources work, some thousands or even hundreds of thousands of samples must be stored.

There are, broadly speaking, two ways in which genetic resources can be conserved, *in situ* and *ex situ*. Conservation *in situ* means the setting aside of natural reserves where the species are allowed to remain in their ecosystems with a minimum of management. The natural biosphere reserve is a useful solution for species that are nearly on the point of extermination (Prescott-Allen, 1981), but for species more widely distributed, the biosphere reserve, which would coincide with only a small part of the total area of a species, could not possibly solve the problem of conserving the total genetic diversity of that species. Similar difficulties pertain to *ex situ* tree orchards or living-plant collections. Only a small fraction can be kept in such collections, since to keep more would involve astronomical costs.

By far the best means of genetic conservation is that of seed storage. Seed stores, known generally as seed banks or gene banks, can hold seed material in large quantities in a relatively small space; the cool rooms of the banks have shelves to hold seed containers. Even the shelving can be mobile, as it is in some laboratories and herbaria, so that less space is needed to gain access to the seeds. Methods have been worked out for optimum storage under conditions of low moisture (2–5%) and low temperature ($+4°$ to $-20°C$, or even lower). The practical details vary, but the usual custom in temperate countries is to cool the chambers and to keep the seeds sealed in moisture-proof receptacles (glass bottles, cans, or foil and plastic packages), well sealed before entry into the storeroom. The normal custom of the seed laboratories is to "equilibrate" the seed to the right moisture content by holding it in an oven and subjecting it to gentle heat, or in a dessicator with air of the correct humidity level. Silica gel is often used as a drying agent, since fortunately it extracts moisture to the correct level (Roberts, 1975).

Harrington (1970) and Roberts (1975) noted that each 1% loss of seed moisture below 14% doubles the life of many seeds. This rule applies down to levels of 4% seed moisture, and Harrington gives the example that onion seeds at 4% last about 1,000 times longer than at 14%. Below 4%, seeds tend to degenerate through autoxidation of lipids in the embryo cells. Again, this effect is not so marked at lower temperatures. Seed survival is even quite good at liquid nitrogen temperatures, always providing that the seeds are fairly dry and the correct conditions of cooling and rewarming are observed (Sakai and Noshiro, 1975; Mumford and Grout, 1978, 1979). These storage methods work well for what Roberts (1973, 1975) calls "orthodox" seeds, where storage lives of up to 50 or even 100 years or more may be possible. They do not, however, work at all for another group, which Roberts calls "recalcitrant."

This group of recalcitrant seeds contains many tropical and subtropical fruit trees and important economic crops such as coffee, cacao, citrus, rubber, and many palms, including oil palm and coconut. Their seeds die very quickly if they are allowed to dry out or cool down toward 0°C, and until now, no certain methods for storing such seeds have been devised. Storage of fully imbibed seeds, that is, those that have taken up a maximum amount of water, has been discussed by Villiers (1975) and may possibly help to solve the problem (Edwards, 1981). The problem of recalcitrant seed storage is particularly galling to many countries in the tropics whose important genetic resources contain a high proportion of species with seeds of this type (Chin and Roberts, 1980). The only way to conserve these species at present is through orchard plantings or in natural reserves, and perhaps by means of meristem cultures. Full imbibition, carefully controlled drying, different gaseous conditions, or even perhaps seedling storage may provide useful results in the future.

Some attention has been paid to pollen storage, which is possible for a few years, but not nearly so long a time as for seeds (Harrington, 1970; Roberts, 1975; Withers, 1980). An added complication is how to reconstitute a plant when only half of the diploid material

Fig. 6.5 Crucifer collection data sheet: (*left*) obverse (*right*) reverse. (IBPGR, 1981c.)

CRUCIFER COLLECTION DATA SHEET

Expedition/Organization (name, year etc): ....

Country: ....

Team/Collector(s): .... *Collector's number:* ....

Date of collection (day/month/year): .... *Photo number(s):* ....

Scientific name (genus, species, subspecies, varietal, in full): ....

....

Common English name: ....

Local crop name: .... *Cultivar name:* ....

Locality (name and address of supplier, and/or number of kilometres and direction from nearest town or village; or map grid reference):

....

....

Traditional name of farming area: ....

Latitude: ....° ....' *Longitude:* ....° ....' *Altitude:* .... m.

Source: 1 Wild   2 Farmer/grower   3 Plant breeder   4 Market   5 Seed firm   6 Genebank

Status: 1 Wild   2 Landrace   3 Cultivar   4 Breeding material   5 Genetic material

Material: Seeds   Herbarium

Sample type: 1 Population   2 Pure line   *Number of plants sampled:* ....

Distance from cross-pollinating crops: .... m.

Normal sowing season:	1 Spring	2 Summer	3 Autumn	4 Winter	5 All year round

Normal harvesting season:	1 Spring 2 Summer 3 Autumn 4 Winter 5 Autumn/winter
	6 Winter/spring 7 All year round

Organ used as primary product: 1 Siliqua 2 Seed   3 Seedling 4 Inflorescence 5 Apical bud   6 Axillary bud/branch 7 Leaf   8 Stem   9 Hypocotyl and/or root

Organ used as secondary product: 1 Siliqua 2 Seed   3 Seedling 4 Inflorescence 5 Apical bud   6 Axillary bud/branch 7 Leaf   8 Stem   9 Hypocotyl and/or root

Primary crop usage I: 1 Vegetable 2 Oil   3 Forage/fodder   4 Green manure 5 Ornamental

Secondary crop usage I: 1 Vegetable 2 Oil   3 Forage/fodder   4 Green manure 5 Ornamental

Primary crop usage II: 1 Fresh   2 Stored unprocessed   3 Ensiled   4 Sauerkraut   5 Kimchee   6 Other stored processed   7 Condiment   8 Lubricant/fuel oil 9 Vegetable oil   10 Chemical synthesis   11 Meal cake/protein

Secondary crop usage II: 1 Fresh   2 Stored unprocessed   3 Ensiled   4 Sauerkraut   5 Kimchee   6 Other stored processed   7 Condiment   8 Lubricant/fuel oil 9 Vegetable oil   10 Chemical synthesis   11 Meal cake/protein

Collector	*Collector*	*Collector*	*Collector*	*Collector*
No:	*No:*	*No:*	*No:*	*No:*

Wild species and primitive cultivars are mainly used as sources of resistance to pests, diseases, and other environmental stresses. If such resistances occur, they are most likely to have developed in areas which are subject to abnormal environmental stresses, or where particular pests or diseases are prevalent. It therefore greatly increases the breeder's chance of finding resistance if he knows which of these factors occur where each seed stock evolved; he is interested in factors which have repeatedly damaged or stressed plants over many seasons in that general area.

Record and mark which of the following stress factors have repeatedly damaged or stressed plants over many seasons in the general area of collection:

High temperature	High relative humidity
Low temperature	High rainfall
Frost	Drought
High winds	
Soil waterlogging	Sulphur deficiency
Soil salinity	Calcium deficiency
Acid soil (pH <4.0)	Magnesium deficiency
Alkaline soil (pH >8.0)	Molybdenum deficiency
Nitrogen deficiency	Boron deficiency
Phosphorus deficiency	Iron deficiency
Potassium deficiency	
Thrips	Stem and gall weevils
Capsids	Other weevils
White fly	Lepidopteran larvae
Aphids	Leaf miners
Springtails	Midges
Sawflies	Cabbage root fly
Flea beetles	Other diptera
Viruses	White spot
Bacterial rots	White mould
Clubroot	Light leaf spot
Powdery mildew	White blister rust
Downy mildew	Wirestem
Dark leaf spot	Ring spot
Canker	Grey leaf spot
Molluscs	Mammals
Birds	Nematodes

from which it was generated is available in the pollen. However, the pollen can be used to maintain and transfer genetic characters, even though it is at present not so satisfactory for long-term use. Ovule and embryo storage is also envisaged (Withers, 1980).

When seeds approach the end of their viability, they must be "rejuvenated" or "regenerated" by sowing them out to obtain a new seed generation. Roberts (1974) has recommended that when the germination percentage drops below 80 – 85% of the original percentage, the seeds must not be kept any longer or genetic damage may result. Care must be taken to prevent genetic drift, or selection that would alter the genetic amplitude of the population that went into storage. It is wise, therefore, to regenerate the seeds at intervals that are as long as possible, and a good sample of the seeds should be sown, with interplant competition kept to a minimum and with conditions as similar as possible to those of the original habitat.

One may wonder whether it is really necessary to maintain individual samples, considering all the consequent labor of testing separate germinations and regenerations. Allard (1970b) regarded static conservation as impossible, and thought that mass reservoirs, where samples are all combined, or bulked up together, might be a better solution to this problem. However, Marshall and Brown (1975) conclude that, in comparison with individual accessions, mass reservoirs are of little use in preserving variation.

Conservation by means of tissue cultures must also be considered. D'Amato (1975) and others have commented that in vitro callus and suspension cultures are unsuitable for genetic conservation because of the frequent genetic or chromosomal changes that occur in the cultures. On the other hand, meristem cultures, in which the morphogenetic potential of the tissues is maintained, do not appear to suffer such genetic or chromosomal changes (Morel, 1975).

Henshaw (1975, 1979; Henshaw, Stamp, and Westcott, 1980; Henshaw, O'Hara, and Westcott, 1980); and Withers, (1980) have discussed the technical aspects of meristem conservation. Henshaw and his co-workers, in collaboration with the International Potato Center in Peru, have demonstrated the feasability of potato meristem storage. (Westcott et al., 1977; Grout, Westcott, and Henshaw, 1977). Storage of cassava (Manihot) meristems is being investigated also, in collaboration with the International Center for Tropical Agriculture (CIAT) in Colombia (Stamp, 1978). It appears that no apparent genetic changes have taken place in potato materials kept in culture under minimal growth conditions for periods of up to one year (Denton, Westcott, and Ford-Lloyd, 1977).

A further interesting advance is cryopreservation of meristem cultures using liquid nitrogen at a temperature of $-196°C$, described by Bajaj (1977) for cassava, by Seibert (1976) for *Dianthus*, and by Grout and Henshaw (1978, 1980) for potato. Recovery rates are reasonably good, especially for potatoes. Here, then, is an alternative method of storage, not yet perfected in every detail but showing considerable promise for the future, that is already being used for certain crops, especially for vegeculture crops and those with "recalcitrant" seeds.

I have suggested another possible alternative for conserving the genetic material of "recalcitrant" species (1982). Seeds of such species are adapted so that they will germinate quickly in a humid tropical forest, but will then wait as seedlings or young plants until the forest canopy opens, through the death of an older tree or through other natural means. The increased light will then cause them to grow rapidly to the canopy level. It is suggested that this natural mechanism of germination and establishment can be exploited by germinating the recalcitrant seeds in the gene bank and storing the seedlings for long periods under carefully controlled conditions of low light. This method effectively takes advantage of the natural methods for maintaining the propagules of tropical forest trees. It remains to be seen, however, whether this method will be successful under laboratory conditions.

Strategies for Conservation

At the fourth, fifth, and sixth meetings of the FAO Panel of Experts on Plant Exploration and Introduction (FAO, 1970, 1973, 1974; Frankel and Hawkes, 1975), a scheme was established to systematize the operations of seed banks. In those institutes, named Genetic Resources Centers, which nationally or internationally assumed responsibility for genetic conservation, two types of seed banks were proposed.

1. *Base Collections*. These were for long-term storage, in which

the seeds would be maintained under optimum conditions and would not be used as a source for distribution. There would be periodic tests for germination in such collections, and the amount of seed stored would be large enough to satisfy foreseeable demands throughout the life of the sample. Even though subsamples would be used for the germination tests, the bulk of the sample would not be opened until regeneration became necessary.

2. *Active Collections*, for medium-term storage. These would be used for multiplication, distribution, evaluation, and documentation. The active collections could be maintained in the same center as the base collections or could be held elsewhere. The standards for these might not be expected to be as high as for the base collections. Active collections must not be confused with breeders' working collections, which are regarded as being outside the scope of genetic resources centers.

A report of a working committee at FAO (Frankel, Roberts, Hawkes, 1974) advocated "desirable" and "minimal" standards of storage, so that seed banks, whenever possible, would be able to conform at least to the minimal standards and could take steps to meet the desirable requirements in due course. The desirable standards call for storage at $-18°C$ or less in airtight containers and moisture content of the seeds of $5 \pm 1\%$ (based on wet weight). Standby equipment would be installed to maintain such a temperature, or return to it rapidly, should there be a power failure or a breakdown of refrigeration equipment. The minimal standards, on the other hand, recommend storage of seeds having a moisture content of 5–7% at 5°C or less in airtight containers, or storage at 5°C or less in unsealed containers in a room controlled to maintain not more than 20% relative humidity. These standards have now been adopted in various gene banks in different parts of the world.

Evaluation and Documentation of Materials

For the materials held in gene banks to be of any value to the breeder, they obviously need to be evaluated. Some seed banks exist where evaluation is very inadequate, and some where it is taken to an extreme and regarded, wrongly, as an end in itself.

For evaluation to be of the greatest use it must be related to breeders' needs. No useful purpose will be served otherwise. However, it cannot be too strongly emphasized that if material is not found to contain the characters desired, *it should not on any account be discarded.* In the past, when breeders looked after their own material, sometimes collected at great expense, they discarded anything that did not satisfy their immediate needs. The object of genetic resources centers is to prevent such action, since we cannot tell what our future needs may be. When I look back on my work with potatoes over some 20 or 30 years, I now know that much of what I regard as interesting and important today was then regarded as of little or no consequence. How can we be certain of what we shall need in 30 years' time, when the material will have disappeared from the farmers' fields completely and can be found only in the gene bank, always assuming that we have been wise enough to preserve it?

Results of screening samples can overwhelm us with the amount of information obtainable. When different laboratories carry out parallel screenings, and when plant breeders, perhaps in other countries, need to know the value of the gene bank collections, only computer held information stores will be large and flexible enough to be of value. The primary collection data that I mentioned earlier must also be available, so that a breeder can check the provenance of his useful material and ask for more from the same region or species if he wishes.

In the past it was possible to exchange such information through correspondence and seed inventories that incorporated the results of screening, but this is becoming impossible, owing to the larger number of collections now in existence. Data-management systems can be of many different types, so long as they are flexible, reasonably mutually compatible, and suited to the mini- or microcomputers now being used (Ford-Lloyd, in Hughes, 1978). Of greater importance, though is that the way of setting out and standardizing the information by means of "descriptors" (characters) and "descriptor states" (character states) should be universally adopted (Rogers, Snoad, and Seidewitz, 1975). Minimal descriptor lists for a wide range of crops have now been published by IBPGR, and more are on their way. The genetic-resources information system can be regarded as the penultimate link in a chain of ongoing activities to conserve genetic material. The ultimate link, on which the existence of all the others depends, is the utilization of the broad spectrum of genetic variability still available to us, to breed better varieties of plants for the future.

7

Global Strategies for Conserving and Utilizing the Genetic Heritage of Plants

The solutions to the problem of genetic erosion are based on solid foundations of genetics, ecology, botany, plant physiology, and computer science, though much research is still needed. I have described the scientific activities now developing, but I have left the organizational and administrative aspects until now. One may wonder why scientists have bothered to become involved in activities that to many seem akin to politics. However, it seems clear that without a solid foundation of leaders and administrators well versed in applied and pure biology, action of the sort that is needed to save our genetic resources is doomed to failure. It is essential, therefore, that scientists should assume their social responsibilities and play a central role in the entire operation.

FAO and Genetic Conservation

Awareness of the dangers of genetic erosion hardly began to develop until after the Second World War. Before that time, the ancient centers of diversity had barely been touched, though much erosion of the old land races outside the centers of diversity in Europe and North America must have been going on long before then. The late H. V. Harlan was perhaps the first to express alarm at the depletion of genetic resources when he said in 1936 (Harlan and

Martini), "In the hinterlands of Asia there were probably barley fields when man was young. The progenies of these fields with all their surviving variations constitute the world's priceless reservoir of germplasm . . . Unfortunately, from the breeder's standpoint it is now being imperiled. When new barleys replace those grown by the farmers of Ethiopia or Tibet, the world will have lost something irreplaceable." We are now realizing only too well how prophetic that statement was.

FAO's interest in genetic resources began in 1947, when the Subcommittee on Plant and Animal Stocks recommended the organization of a clearing-house for information and for a free interchange of plant materials throughout the world (Whyte, 1958). In 1961, the FAO Division of Plant Production and Protection held a technical meeting on plant exploration and introduction that reviewed the world situation and made useful suggestions and recommendations (FAO, 1961). The meeting suggested that "exploration centers" be established in various parts of the world so that useful material could be assembled and studied in the centers of diversity with ease and efficiency. The FAO Crop Research and Introduction Center, then shortly to be established at Izmir, Turkey, was considered highly suitable for that purpose.

An important further recommendation was that a special office or service be established at FAO to act as a focus of interest and activity in germplasm work and that the office should be advised by an independent panel of experts. Although such a panel was established in 1965, it was not called to advise until after the second technical conference convened in 1967.

In that year, FAO and the International Biological Program (IBP) jointly convened a "Technical Conference on the Exploration, Utilization, and Conservation of Plant Genetic Resources" at FAO headquarters in Rome (FAO, 1967; Bennett, 1968). Again, many recommendations were made, and a valuable book (Frankel and Bennett, 1970) was published, based on the papers read at the conference. This was the first major attempt, apart from the report on the 1961 conference, to put together a wide range of ideas related to the complete field of endeavors to preserve genetic resources. The very phrase "genetic resources" was invented at that time, and from then on, genetic conservation took its place as a biological discipline through the synthesis of topics from other biological fields.

A third technical conference was held at Rome in 1973, again convened jointly by FAO and IBP. It was organized by the Chairman of the Panel of Experts, Sir Otto Frankel, and also by other members of the panel and of the Unit for Crop Ecology and Genetic Resources. A volume based on this conference was published by IBP (Frankel and Hawkes, 1975) as part of a series of "synthesis volumes" resulting from the ten years of IBP's activities. In this work the scientific bases of exploration, sampling, evaluation, seed and tissue culture conservation, and documentation and information management were covered in depth. It thus tied in with the first volume and showed the progress achieved in the intervening years. A further technical conference was organized in 1981 by FAO and the International Board for Plant Genetic Resources (IBPGR). A volume dealing with the topics discussed at this conference will also be published.

In 1957 FAO also began to issue *Plant Introduction Newsletter*, concerned chiefly with the listing of collections of crop germplasm available in different parts of the world. In 1971, the newsletter was given an improved format and a new name, the *Plant Genetic Resources Newsletter*. For a number of years it was edited by Erna Bennett of FAO but has now been taken over by IBPGR and is edited by Dr. J. T. Williams. It has become the accepted vehicle for news and views on all aspects of genetic resources activities throughout the world.

The FAO Unit of Crop Ecology and Genetic Resources was established in 1968 to act as a clearing-house for information on collections and expeditions and to encourage initiatives wherever possible. Two expert panels were also set up, one in 1967 (FAO, 1968) on the genetic resources of forest plants, and one on those of crop plants, in 1965. Each panel was composed of appropriate experts from various countries. The Panel of Experts on Plant Exploration and Introduction produced its most important reports at its third, fourth, fifth, and sixth sessions (See FAO, 1969, 1970, 1973, and 1974); it has not met since 1974.

The panel's third session in 1969 looked at the problem of genetic erosion in various parts of the world and made recommendations for conducting surveys, setting priorities for exploration in regions most under threat, providing of funds for such work, and for training the necessary personnel. At that meeting I was able to announce the foundation of a training course at the University of Birmingham that I shall describe below. The priorities recommended for collection in the Near East, the Sahelian zone of West Africa, Ethiopia, and certain other areas, together with the endangered crops for each region, were especially important.

At its fourth session, in 1970, the panel established in considerable detail the definitions and functions of genetic resources centers, and it redefined priorities for crop and regional exploration. It then turned its attention to the problem of genetic information and data processing. The panel noted the work of FAO and the International Atomic Energy Agency at Vienna in convening a meeting on this topic in 1965, and it recommended standard data formats, appropriate computer programming, and the establishment of an international information center to bring this about. It further recommended to FAO that an information storage and retrieval system be established within the Unit of Crop Ecology and Genetic Resources.

The fifth session of the panel of experts took place in 1973, just before the third technical conference, which the panel had previously recommended. This session reemphasized the recommendations made earlier and drew attention to the findings of the Beltsville Report (which I shall discuss later). It also redefined and clarified the functions of base and active collections in the genetic resources centers and pointed out for exploration three "target areas" where emergencies had arisen through very rapid genetic erosion. These areas were:

1. The Near East and Mediterranean region, where the situations for wheat, oats, rye, grain legumes, melons, and vegetables, and their wild relatives was critical. Cooperation between genetic resources centers in Turkey and Italy was urgently recommended, and appropriate funding was suggested.
2. Ethiopia, where wheat was the most endangered crop; barley, coffee, grain legumes, vegetables, sorghum, and millets, were also listed as needing instant attention.
3. Tropical areas in Meso- and South America, Southeast Asia, and tropical West Africa, where many crops were described as threatened, including Asian and African rice, grain legumes, root crops, tree fruits, small grains, vegetables, and forage grasses.

Again, the panel stressed the urgency of establishing various types of training courses.

At the sixth session, which met in 1974 after the International Board for Plant Genetic Resources was established, the panel felt that it should continue to act in an advisory capacity to FAO and to the board by providing scientific and technical recommendations as it had done previously. It again discussed training, crop and regional priorities in exploration, and the question of storage. Surveys of facilities in established gene banks provided a clearer picture of the capacity for storage throughout the world and of the technical levels of the various banks. The panel's review has stimulated discussion in gene banks in all parts of the world. A working group of the panel (Roberts, 1974) had recommended conditions for seed storage earlier that year, and the review included details of costs and regeneration intervals as well.

Although it is true that the panel and its individual members, together with members of the Unit for Crop Ecology and Genetic Resources, provided all the scientific initiatives and theoretical bases for genetic resources development for some ten years, the panel was able to accomplish very little in practical terms. This was mainly owing to the lack of financial support on the part of FAO, and, in consequence, very little was brought about by FAO itself. The initiative for development has now completely passed to the International Board for Plant Genetic Resources. However, FAO and its panel of experts was able to do much by its appeals and its publications, so that the time was not really lost. Foundations were laid and plans and activities were developed by the panel and by many other bodies.

The Consultative Group on International Agricultural Research (CGIAR)

The CGIAR, which was established in 1971 under joint sponsorship of the World Bank, FAO, and the United Nations Development Program (UNDP), is funded by private foundations such as the Ford, Rockefeller, and Kellog Foundations, by the UNDP, by regional development programs, and by donor countries, through the World Bank. CGIAR seeks to increase food production in the developing world through research programs and the training of research and extension scientists in the developing nations. In 1972 the funding was some $15 million; in 1976 it had increased to $64 million (CGIAR, 1976). Research is undertaken through seven research institutes or centers for crops and two for animals, the West African Rice Development Association, the International Board for Plant Genetic Resources, and some other offices.

In 1971 the Technical Advisory Committee (TAC) was established to assist CGIAR. In 1972, TAC, together with FAO, sponsored an ad hoc working group in Beltsville, Maryland, on the collection, evaluation, and conservation of plant genetic resources. The report of this working group, revised by TAC in 1973, set out a blueprint for genetic resources work. World efforts were to be partitioned into ten regions based roughly on Vavilov's centers of diversity in crop plants (refer back to Figure 3.1 and Table 3.1). The regions proposed were China; India; Southeast Asia; the Mediterranean, Near East, and the Middle East; Ethiopia and East Africa; tropical Africa; Meso-America; Central America and lowland, tropical South America; the Andean highlands; and subtropical to temperate South America. For each region a regional center would be designated to coordinate the work of the countries within the region; it would establish facilities for long-term seed conservation, as well as information storage and retrieval services. Crop priorities were drawn up for each of the regions, and the CGIAR network was included in the general plan. This blueprint was useful, because it established a basis for a world scheme where financial support might be forthcoming.

In the same year, 1972, the United Nations Environment Conference took place at Stockholm, where the matter of conserving genetic resources was discussed and agreed to without any dissent. The subsequently established United Nations Environment Program, based in Nairobi, Kenya, provided much funding for activities concerning genetic resources from 1974 onward.

The International Board for Plant Genetic Resources (IBPGR)

In 1973 the Consultative Group on International Agricultural Research, having agreed to the main points set out by the Beltsville Working Group, agreed with FAO to establish a body to stimulate and coordinate genetic resources activities throughout the world, that would have status similar to that of the CGIAR research center but with a secretariat at FAO (and no permanent headquarters other than that of the secretariat). Members were chosen on the basis of scientific interests and geographic background and were to meet once a year. This was the International Board for Plant Genetic Resources, which first met in June, 1974. At that meeting it agreed to continue or establish regional programs and to approve the Genetic Resources Communication and Documentation System established by Dr. David Rogers of the University of Colorado (IBPGR, 1974). In 1975 it established a more detailed series of priorities for crops and for regions, suggesting fourteen regions, rather than the ten recommended at Beltsville. The regions were based very closely on the Vavilovian centers of diversity, with the addition of four others: the Pacific Islands, East Africa, West Africa, and subtropical South America and the deletion of Vavilov's Chilean Center.

In 1976 (*IBPGR News Bulletin*, July 1976a) crop advisory committees had been established for rice, maize, wheat, sorghum, and millets and *Phaseolus* beans, and a working group on coconut was set up. Attention was also focused on tropical fruits, vegetables, bananas, and groundnuts, as well as on problems of storage, quarantine, training, exploration and information systems. Regional programs had been agreed upon for Europe (with the European Association for Research on Plant Breeding – EUCARPIA – and UNDP), the Mediterranean (with the Italian Germplasm Laboratory at Bari), southwestern Asia, Southeast Asia, southern Asia, Costa Rica, and Africa (in collaboration with the International Institute of Tropical Agriculture, Ibadan, Nigeria). The concept of having centrally controlled regional networks had changed a great deal since the Beltsville Report. The tendency now was to form regional associations of countries, with an IBPGR regional coordinator, rather than a single country, to guide the work. This idea of an association of equal partners has gathered momentum, particularly in Southeast Asia, southwestern Asia, southern Asia, and the Mediterranean basin.

Perhaps one of the most important tasks of the board has been the funding of exploration work in various parts of the world, especially in the high-priority regions of the Mediterranean and Near East, and the Sahelian zone of West Africa. It has also given considerable support to the Southeast Asian network in the planning of conferences and committees (see, for example, Williams et al., 1975) and has recently commissioned another bibliography of plant genetic resources (Hawkes, Williams, and Hanson, 1976; Williams, 1977). The board has discussed documentation and information systems (IBPGR Advisory Committee, 1976b) and a survey on engineering designs and costs for long-term storage facilities was published (IBPGR, 1976c).

By 1981, IBPGR, through the insight and perseverance of its Executive Secretary Dr. J. T. Williams, had clearly made a major impact on genetic resources activities (IBPGR, 1981). Working in close association with FAO, it has had a dramatic catalytic effect on the conservation work of scientists and agricultural centers throughout the world. By carefully using available funding, it has been able to coordinate existing efforts and to promote new ones in the general area of collection, conservation, and evaluation of plant genetic resources. It has arranged conferences, working groups, and training courses, has encouraged the availability of material for plant breeding, and has established standards for collecting, storing, evaluating, and documenting the genetic materials.

Furthermore, in the short span of seven years, it has published a manual on crop exploration and directories of germplasm collections of root crops, food legumes, wheat, maize, rice, sorghum, and millets. Booklets have been published on the genetic resources of amaranths, bananas and plantains, cocoa, coconuts, coffee, cruciferous crops, sweet potato, tomatoes, tropical vegetables, and wheat. In addition, it has published lists of descriptors and descriptor states for the uniform documentation of genetic resources in gene banks and other collections of almond, apricot, beets, *Colocasia*, cotton, cultivated potatoes, groundnuts, maize, mung bean, pearl millet, pigeon pea, rice, *Sesame*, *Sorghum*, tropical fruits (and a revised edition on them), wheat (and a revised edition), wheat and *Aegilops*, winged bean, and yams. These publications are so numerous that I have not included them in the bibliography. They may be obtained by writing to the IBPGR at FAO, in Rome.

IBPGR has continued and greatly extended the work of the FAO panel of experts in the designation of priority crops and priority regions for the collection and conservation of the world's genetic resources. To begin with, emphasis was placed on the major food crops, but by 1981 over 50 crops were assigned first-priority status, either globally or in certain countries or regions. Regions have also been accorded priorities (Fig. 7.1 and the Appendix).

Priority 1 region spreads eastward in a broad belt from the western Mediterranean countries through the Near East, Ethiopia, and southwestern Asia to India and surrounding countries. It also includes most of Mexico, Central America, the Guianas and the Caribbean. Priority 2 region comprises the northern and central Andean countries of South America, Brazil, West and central Africa, and East and Southeast Asian countries as far as New Guinea. Priority 3 region includes most of the temperate and warm temperate parts of South America, a broad belt in Africa running along the eastern side from Sudan to Botswana, and Mozambique and Madagascar. It also includes the whole of Oceania. Little by little, since the work has become so vast, regional officers are being appointed to the main regions, and the formation of regional communities is being extended.

It is clear, therefore, that the program of IBPGR, with the funding that it can command from the World Bank through CGIAR, has been able to accomplish a great deal in a remarkably short time. The ideas and priorities established by the FAO panel of experts and the Beltsville Report have been greatly strengthened and much extended, bringing in national and international organizations, existing institutes, and expertise wherever they can be found. In particular, IBPGR has made use of the CGIAR centers network, as has been mentioned before.

The Centers Network of CGIAR

The crop-research centers have developed germplasm exploration, conservation, and utilization programs as follows (Fig. 7.2):

1. *The International Rice Institute* (IRRI), Los Baños, Philippines, obviously focuses on rice, and considerable collections have been assembled of cultivars from throughout southern, southeastern, and eastern Asia; work is continuing on indigenous varieties and populations of cultivated rice, and particularly of wild rice species, in Asia and Africa. It stores *indica* and *javanica* rices; the West African rices are stored at the International Institute of

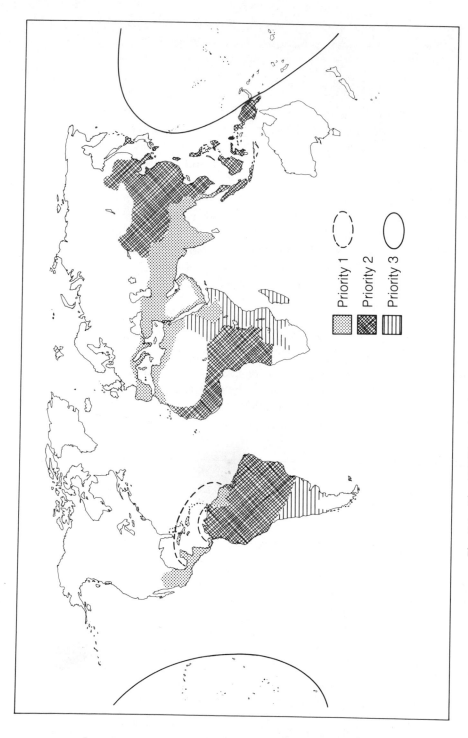

Fig. 7.1 The IBPGR regional priorities as of 1981. (IBPGR, 1981b.)

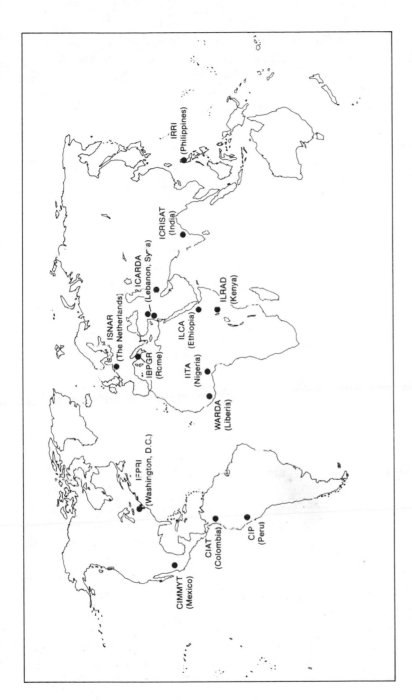

Fig. 7.2 The CGIAR network. For explanation see text and Abbreviations (CGIAR, 1980.)

Tropical Agriculture, and the *japonica* ones are stored in Japan.

2. *The International Maize and Wheat Improvement Center* (CIMMYT), El Batán, Mexico, has a very large collection of maize material, but much is held in local collections. Wheat is held elsewhere, though CIMMYT assumes general responsibility for breeding research on wheat germplasm.

3. *The International Center for Tropical Agriculture* (CIAT), Palmira, Colombia, has taken responsibility for the germplasm of *Manihot* (cassava), *Phaseolus* beans, and tropical forage grasses and legumes. Collections are available and more collecting work is in progress.

4. *The International Institute of Tropical Agriculture* (IITA), Ibadan, Nigeria, is responsible for genetic resources of African rice, root crops, cowpea, tropical groundnuts, and other regional crops (except sorghum and millet). Its interests are not confined only to West Africa but extend into other parts of that continent as well.

5. *The International Potato Center* (CIP), Lima, Peru, established a germplasm exploration program in 1973 and has already reached its target of assembling some 12,000 lines of primitive cultivated forms of potatoes from the Andes and southern Chile. It is now concentrating upon the wild species.

6. *The International Crop Research Institute for the Semi-Arid Tropics* (ICRISAT), Hyderabad, India, as its name implies, has as its principal genetic resources objectives the assembling of germplasm of drought-resisting materials, chiefly sorghum, millets, chickpea, groundnut, and pigeon pea.

7. *The International Center for Agricultural Research on Dry Areas (ICARDA), Aleppo, Syria, and Beirut, Lebanon, is concerned with Mediterranean and Near Eastern crops adapted to dry regions — for example, barley, lentils, Vicia (worldwide), durum wheat, and chickpea (regional).*

8. *The Asian Vegetable Research Development Center* (AVRDC), Taiwan, is loosely associated with the CGIAR network but is not officially part of it. It is responsible for tomato, soybean, Chinese cabbage, sweet potato, mung bean, and several other vegetable crops.

9. *The West African Rice Development Association* is also associated with then CGIAR network, but does not have responsibilities for germplasm conservation.

The integration of the germplasm activities of these international crop research centers and institutes into the global genetic resources network was clearly foreseen by the writers of the Beltsville Report, and several institutes (IRRI, CIMMYT, CIP) had already initiated such collections. However, the difference in outlook between the center network and the regional network is of interest in that the centers "slice the cake" vertically by crops, while the regions slice it horizontally by geographical areas. Overlap is minimal, and sufficient consultation takes place to render what overlap that does occur useful and complementary.

The Regional Networks

Most of the work of establishing the regional networks has been the responsibility of IBPGR. These are as follows:

1. *Europe*. Work on genetic resources has been in existence in Europe, of course, since the first collections of Vavilov and his colleagues were established at the Institute of Plant Industry in Leningrad (Brezhnev, 1970, 1975), but through the initiatives in 1961 of the European Association for Research on Plant Breeding (EUCARPIA) a gene bank committee was later established (Hawkes and Lamberts, 1977). A network of banks for European genetic resources was recommended to serve the needs of European breeders, based on the main agroecological regions, as follows:

The Istituto del Germoplasma, in Bari, southern Italy, has responsibility for southern European and Mediterranean crops, especially durum wheats, and is now linked to IBPGR as the main coordinating center for the Mediterranean region.

The Gene Bank, Institut für Pflanzenbau und Pflanzenzüchtung in Braunschweig-Völkenrode, West Germany, deals with crops of central to northwestern Europe. It also contains the collaborative Dutch and German potato gene bank which is likely to be extended when other countries join in.

The Nordic Gene Bank in Lund, Sweden, is funded and organized cooperatively by the five Nordic countries, Sweden, Norway, Denmark, Finland, and Iceland; it takes responsibility for crops of the Far North.

In England, the seed bank at Kew is concerned with seeds of wild species only, while the main responsibilities of the Vegetable Gene Bank at the National Vegetable Research Station, in Wellesbourne, are *Brassica* crops and onions (*Allium*).

It is of interest to note that the first four banks mentioned above were established by national governments on the recommendation of EUCARPIA. Other western European banks now established are in Braga, Portugal; Madrid, Spain; Thessaloniki, Greece; Nicosia, Cyprus; Wageningen, Holland; Gembloux, Belgium; and Montpellier, France.

In 1975 the EUCARPIA Gene Bank Committee set up a working group to integrate the western European network with the one in Eastern Europe. Further support and funding has been made available by UNDP recently for the European regional program. The Eastern European banks include the N. I. Vavilov Institute of Plant Industry in Leningrad, which contains a very extensive collection of temperate and subtropical crops and has been in existence since Vavilov's time. Other banks are being developed in Gatersleben, East Germany, which was established some time ago and possesses an excellent range of collections; Radzikow, Poland; Prague, Czechoslovakia; Tapioszele, Hungary; Fundulea, Romania; and Plovdiv, Bulgaria.

2. *Southeast Asia* (Indonesia, Malaysia, Thailand, Singapore, the Philippines, and Papua–New Guinea). The Network committee has met several times to recommend priorities and national responsibilities for field crops and fruit trees.

3. *Southwest Asia* (Turkey, Syria, Iraq, Iran, Afghanistan, and Pakistan). Wheats, barley, rye, grain legumes (chickpea, lentil, *Vicia*, pea), and some other crops have received high- to medium-priority ratings.

4. *South Asia* (India, Sri Lanka, Burma, Nepal, and Bhutan). This network works with temperate and tropical cereals and grains, fruits, vegetables, spices, and medicinal plants. There is a large national program in India (the National Bureau of Plant Genetic Resources).

5. *The Mediterranean Region* (Algeria, Cyprus, Egypt, Greece, Italy, Lybia, Portugal, Spain, Tunisia, and Yugoslavia). All the main regional crops, especially durum wheats, are considered.

6. Other regional programs (in Africa, the Andean zone, Meso-America, for example) are still under discussion and development.

National Programs

In Europe, apart from UNDP and IBPGR help, all programs are nationally funded. Some of the network connections and smaller regions are supported partly by national and partly by international funds. Up to now, I have made little mention of the substantial work in germplasm exploration and conservation that has been successfully undertaken by the United States government.

As Harlan (1975a) points out, agriculture in the United States is imported, and so are its crops. Thus, coordinated plant introduction began as far back as 1819, and by 1898 a section of Seed and Plant Introduction Division was established in the Department of Agriculture that has since developed into the well-known Plant Introduction Service of the USDA (Hyland, 1970, 1975). This led to the establishment of the four regional Plant Introduction Stations (1947–1952) and of the Interregional Potato Introduction Station in 1949. An extremely valuable step was taken in 1958 when the National Seed Storage Laboratory in Fort Collins, Colorado, was set up; by 1975 it had 83,000 accessions. A total of nearly 400,000 accessions has been registered by the USDA since 1898. Of course, not all these accessions are still in existence, but Hyland reports that some 60–75% are still viable.

Special collections of wheat, barley, oats, and rye (60,000 accessions), beans (61,000), peanuts (3,800), tomato (3,500), sorghum (3,400), and a range of other crops are preserved and are being utilized in the four regions. Even so, much genetic diversity is still required, and plant collectors are still sampling crops in various parts of the world. Nevertheless, Harlan points out that there are no grounds for complacency, since the genetic base in maize is dangerously narrow (National Academy of Sciences, 1972), and that of peanuts is also vulnerable. The Southern corn leaf-blight epidemic of 1970 showed the risks quite clearly, and consequently, the Agricultural Research Policy Advisory Committee agreed in 1975 to a recommendation for the establishment of a National Genetic Resources Board. Thus there is now an official awareness of the problems of the erosion of genetic resources in the United States, and the government is helping international conservation efforts generously.

A large national program known as CENARGEN was recently established in Brazil, with base collections as well as information storage in Brasilia. Active collections are established in breeding institutes in other parts of the country. Valuable genetic-resources programs have also been established in Canada, Australia, Japan, China, Israel, and elsewhere. The materials in the Japanese bank are being conserved under first-class conditions, but unfortunately, space space do not permit detailed descriptions of any of the national gene banks.

Training

Training personnel competent in working with genetic resources has been regarded as extremely important for some time. The third session of the FAO panel of experts (FAO, 1969) gave full and enthusiastic support to the proposals of Birmingham University (England), for an international training course leading to the degree of Master of Science. This course, entitled "Conservation and Utilisation of Plant Genetic Resources," has now been running for over a decade, and a total of some 150 students from 45 countries, most of them from the developing world, have received training there (Hawkes and Williams, 1976). Some of these students have also continued their studies for the degree of Ph.D. Since 1975, funding from IBPGR has supported the training of up to 15 students from developing countries per year.

Including the one-year Master of Science course, the FAO panel of experts agreed to recommend five types of training:

1. *Short, practical courses,* lasting four to six weeks, to provide a training in the practice of Seed banking, tissue culture, documentation and data management, and field-collecting techniques. Field-exploration courses have been organized at Bogor, Indonesia, as well as at New Delhi, India; IITA, Nigeria; and Pergamino, Argentina. Courses in genetic resources are also taking place at Lima, Peru. Short courses on data management have been held at Boulder, Colorado, and in Bari, Italy. Postgraduate options in genetic resources are now offered in various universities (for example, in Ames, Iowa; and in New Delhi, India). It is hoped that training courses on the other topics mentioned will be available shortly.
2. *Medium-length courses* lasting three months would provide more extensive training for scientists in particular aspects of a subject at both theoretical and practical levels. Two modular sections of the Birmingham M.Sc. course are offered for three-month periods of specialized training. Topics include crop plant diversity, its

exploration and conservation, Genetic resources evaluation and utilization, and data preparation and management.

3. *The Master of Science in Genetic Resources* lasting 12 months has already been discussed.

4. *The Ph.D. in Genetic Resources* lasting three to four years has also been mentioned. Many students registered at Birmingham University for a Ph.D. study for at least two, and sometimes three, years at their own institutes or at one of the International Crop Centers. Other universities offer similar opportunities.

5. *High-level refresher courses* lasting one to three weeks might be arranged from time to time either at universities or at crop research institutes where germplasm and related plant-breeding studies are in progress. A workshop held several years ago at the N. I. Vavilov Institute of Plant Industry was an excellent example of this kind of course, organized jointly by the Institute and FAO.

A point to note is that although most of the courses have begun in developed countries, the trend is to move them to developing countries wherever possible. The CGIAR Centers Network can obviously play an important role, because they already have much experience in providing training courses of many different types.

Conclusion

I have tried to trace the complex interweaving and overlapping of the meetings, activities, and responsibilities, of agencies, boards, and committees that have been established in many parts of the world and that have gathered such momentum in the last seven or eight years that most of them have been taking place almost simultaneously. The situation is complex, but I hope that I have said enough about it to persuade the reader that a tremendous effort is being made to conserve the genetic diversity of crop plants and to bring it to the notice of the breeders. Those of us who have been involved in this work have found it both frustrating and invigorating. Lack of funds or bureaucratic delays have provided frustrations enough, but these have been fully compensated for by the elation and satisfaction of seeing one more positive step taken, one more piece fitted into the jigsaw puzzle.

What of the future? How long do we need to conserve our genetic heritage before some more refined way of mutation breeding or genetic engineering takes its place? Are we conserving everything we shall need for the future? As far as the genetic resources of cultigens are concerned, the answer is probably that we are doing as much as humanly possible, but when it comes to wild species, we connot really be certain. Hegnauer (1975) has struck a rather pessimistic note by giving examples of wild taxa that, but for chance, might have disappeared completely, taking their valuable qualities with them.

Wild species may possibly be sources of future food, but the likelihood is that we have domesticated more than we need in that direction. More probably we shall need our wild species to provide resistances to disease and pests, or secondary metabolites that cannot be completely synthesized in the laboratory. Only time will tell, but meanwhile we would be wise to conserve as much as we reasonably can, both in natural reserves and in germplasm banks.

The lesson we have all been learning in the last ten years is to conserve as much as or more than we consider to be essential for the present. We should plan for the next 30 to 50 years, so that even if our forecasts have not been completely accurate, at least our children and our grandchildren will not be able to accuse us of rejecting our responsibilities of preserving the diversity of our biological heritage. We have also learned that conservation and agricultural development are not irreconcilable. After all, most of the diversity of our cultivated plants has developed *because* of man, not in opposition to him. We should be able to do as well in the future, not only by developing new strains of better-yielding, resistant, and adapted cultigens but also by learning more from the past and by increasing, rather than diminishing, the genetic diversity of plants.

Appendix

IBPGR Revised Priorities for Crops and Regions (Including, with the Name of the Crop, Wild and Cultivated Genera and Species). (IBPGR, 1981b)

Priority S indicates crops needing further study

CROP PRIORITIES

Cereals

Priority 1

Wheat	Although much collecting has been carried out, material still remains to be collected in the Mediterranean, southwestern Asia, and the Himalayas.

Priority 2

Sorghum	In view of the sizable collections assembled at ICRISAT from tropical Africa, priority 2 seems appropriate. However, wild races of sorghum continue to have priority 1 throughout Africa, and cultivated sorghums from West Africa, China, and parts of Southeast Asia remain priority 1.
Pearl millet (*Pennisetum*)	In view of the work carried out in 1976–1980, priority 2 seems appropriate. Nonetheless, pearl millet is a priority 1 in Chad, North Africa, and parts of India and Pakistan.

CEREALS (cont.)

Finger millet (*Eleusine*)	Priority 1 in Africa and Asia.
Foxtail millet (*Setaria italica*)	*Priority 1 in China.*
Fonio millet (*Digitaria* sp.)	———
Rice	Because of the outstanding work of IRRI, especially in Asia, priority 2 seems appropriate for rice in general, but collections of rice in tribal areas in India, Indochina, China, and the Pacific have priority 1.
Barley	Priority 1 in China, southwestern Asia, and North Africa.

Priority 3

Maize	Priority 1 in the Himalayas, China, and northeastern Brazil, Venezuela, and the Guyanas.
Grain Amaranth	Priority 2 in the Andean zone.
Oats	———
Quinoa	Priority 1 in the Andean zone.
Rye	———
Proso millet or common millet (*Panicum miliaceum*)	———
Barnyard millet (*Echnichloa crus-galli*)	———

Priority 4

Teff (*Eragostis*)	High local priority.
Kodo millet (*Paspalum scrobiculatum*)	High local priority.
Little millet (*Panicum miliare*)	High local priority.

Food Legumes (*including vegetable types where applicable*)

Priority 1

Phaseolus beans	A broader range of genetic diversity is required for breeding programs. In addition, agricultural land-use patterns are changing rapidly in Central and South America, which may lead to the disappearance of many traditional cultivars of *Phaseolus*.

Priority 2

Groundnut	Priority 1 in southern Asia, Southeast Asia, and Central America.
Soybean	Priority 1 in China, Indonesia, and parts of Southeast Asia.
Cowpea (*Vigna unguiculata*)	Priority 1 in southern Asia and West Africa.
Yardlong bean (*Vigna unguiculata* spp. *sesquipedalis*)	Priority 1 in Southeast Asia.
Winged bean (*Psophocarpus tetragonolobus*)	Priority 1 in the Pacific and southern and Southeast Asia.
Chickpea	Priority 1 in Southwest Asia.
Greengram (*Vigna radiata*)	Priority 1 in southern and Southeast Asia.
Blackgram (*Vigna mungo*)	Priority 1 in southern and Southeast Asia.
Moth bean (*Vigna aconitifolia*)	———
Rice bean (*Vigna umbellata*)	———

Priority 3

Pigeon pea (*Cajanus*)	———
Pea (*Pisum*)	———
Broad bean (*Vica faba*)	Priority 1 in the Mediterranean.
Lentil	Priority 1 in southwestern Asia.

FOOD LEGUMES (cont.)

Bambara groundnut (*Voandzeia*)	Priority 2 in West Africa.
Vigna angularis	———
Vigna trilobata	———

Priority 4

Lupin	Priority 1 in Andean zone.
Velvet bean (*Mucuna* sp.)	———
Dolichos and *Lablab* spp.	———
Jack bean and sword bean (*Canavalia* spp.)	———
Kersting's groundnut (*Kerstingiella geocarpa*)	———
Cluster bean (*Cyamopsis tetragonoloba*)	———
African yam bean (*Sphenostylis stenocarpa*)	———

Root and Tuber Crops (*including vegetable types where applicable*)

Priority 1

Cassava	———
Sweet potato	———

Priority 2

Potato	Potatoes have a priority 2 because a large amount of material has already been collected and is conserved by CIP.

Priority 3

Yam	Priority 1 in the Pacific.

Priority 4

Taro and aroids	Priority 1 in the Pacific.
Minor South American tuber crops	Priority 1 in Andean zone.
Minor African tuber crops	———

Oil Crops

Priority 2

Oil palm (*Elaeis melanococca*)	*In restricted areas of South America.*
Coconut	Priority 1 in Southeast Asia and the Pacific.
Oil-seed brassicas	Priority 1 in southern Asia and China.

Priority 3

Oil palm (*E. guineensis*)	———
Safflower	———
Sunflower	———
Olive	———

Priority 4

Niger seed (*Guizotia abyssinica*)	———
Sesame	———

Fiber Crops

Priority 2

Cotton	———

Priority 3

Jute	———

Priority 4

Kenaf (*Hibiscus cannabinus*)	———

Priority S

Flax	———
Linseed	———

Starchy Fruits

Priority 2

Starchy banana and plantain	Priority 1 in the Pacific, Southeast Asia, and West Africa.

STARCHY FRUITS (cont.)

Priority 3

Breadfruit and jack-fruit | High priority in southern and Southeast Asia, and priority 1 in Pacific.

Sugar Crops

Priority 2

Sugar beet and related spp. | Beet, in general, has priority 2, but priority 1 is assigned to the genetic resources of *Beta* that are being lost rapidly in parts of Turkey and the Mediterranean.

Sugar cane | Priority 1 in the Pacific, southern and Southeast Asia.

Rubber

Priority 2

Rubber (*Hevea brasiliensis*) | New germplasm is required to provide varieties resistant to South American leaf-blight disease (SALB). With increased and improved communication between Latin American and Asian and African regions, spread of this disease is almost a certainty. Furthermore, fear of accidental introduction of SALB from the Brazilian forest regions into the main areas of production in Africa and Asia has to date limited plant exploration activity.

Beverages

Priority 1

Coffee | New germplasm is needed of *Coffea arabica* because of coffee-berry disease and coffee rust. Clearing in West Africa may similarly lessen the availability of genetic diversity of *C. canephora* in that region.

BEVERAGES (cont.)

Priority 2

Cocoa   The development of the Amazon region is reduc-
                    ing genetically diverse cocoa material that will be
                    most useful in breeding for disease resistance and
                    higher yields. Cocoa is an important shareholders'
                    crop for a major portion of their export earnings.
                    In general, the priority is 2, but for *Criollo* va-
                    rieties it is 1, because of the potential of this
                    material.

Priority 4

Tea   ———

Other

Grape   See miscellaneous crops.

Tropical and Subtropical Fruits and Tree Nuts

Priority 2

Dessert banana   Priority 1 in Southeast Asia.

Citrus   Priority 1 in southern and Southeast Asia.

Mango   Priority 1 in Southeast Asia.

Priority 3

Avocado   Priority 1 in Central America and 2 in Andean
                    zone.

Cashew   Priority 2 in southern Asia.

Date   Priority 2 in southwestern Asia.

Fig   Priority 2 in southwestern Asia.

Papaya   Priority 2 in Central America and Andean zone.

Pineapple   ———

Priority 4

Peach palm   Priority 1 in parts of Latin America.

Priority 5

Other tropical fruits   *Lansium*, durian and rambutan, are priority 1 in
and tree nuts   Southeast Asia. *Annona* and *Passiflora* spp. are
                        priority 1 in Andean zone.

Temperate Fruits and Tree Nuts

Priority 2

Apple	Priority 1 in southwestern Asia.
Pear and Quince	Priority 1 in southwestern Asia.
Peach and Nectarine	———

Priority 3

Apricot	Priority 2 in southwestern Asia.
Cherry	Priority 2 in southwestern Asia.
Plum	———
Strawberry	———

Priority 4

Almond	Priority 2 in southwestern Asia.
Walnut	Priority 2 in southwestern Asia.

Priority S

Other temperate fruit and tree nuts	Pomegranate is priority 2 in southwestern Asia.

Vegetables

Priority 1

Tomato (*Lycopersicon esculentum* and related spp.)	———

Priority 2

Amaranth (*Amaranthus* spp.)	Priority 1 in West Africa and southern and Southeast Asia.
Brassicas (*Brassica campestris, B. juncea, B. oleracea*)	Priority 1 in China, southern and southwestern Asia and the Mediterranean.
Cucurbits (*Cucurbita* spp.)	Priority 1 in Latin America
Eggplant (*Solanum melongena* and related spp.)	Priority 1 in southern and Southeast Asia and West Africa.

VEGETABLES (cont.)

Okra (*Abelmoschus esculentus* and related spp.)	Priority 1 in the Pacific
Onion (*Allium* spp.)	Priority 1 in southwestern Asia.
Pepper [Chili] (*Capsicum* spp.)	Priority 1 in Latin America, southern and Southeast Asia.
Radish (*Raphanus sativus* and related spp.)	Priority 1 in southwestern Asia.

Priority 3

Bitter gourd (*Momordica charantia* and related spp.)	Priority 1 in Southeast Asia.
Ethiopian mustard (*Brassica carinata*)	———
Sokoyokoto (*Celosia argentea*)	———
Swede, rapo-kalo (*Brassica rapus*)	
Globe artichoke (*Cynara scolymus*)	High priority in the Mediterranean.

Priority 4

Bottle gourd (*Lagenaria* spp.)	Priority 2 in Latin America.
Carrot (*Daucus carota*)	———
Chaya (*Cnidoscolus chayamansa*)	———
Chayote (*Sechium edule*)	Priority 1 in Central America.
Cucumber, gherkin (*Cucumis sativus*)	———
Fluted pumpkin (*Telfairea*)	———
Indian or Ceylon spinach (*Basella alba*)	———

VEGETABLES (cont.)

Jute mallow (Corchorus olitorius)	———
Kangkong (*Ipomoea aquatica*)	Priority 1 in Southeast Asia.
Lettuce (*Lactuca sativa*)	———
Muskmelon, Cantaloupe (*Cucumis melo*)	Priority 1 in southwestern Asia.
Watermelon (*Citrullus lanatus*)	———
Spinach (*Spinacia oleracea*)	Priority 1 in southwestern Asia.

Miscellaneous Crops

Priority 2

Trees for fuel wood and environmental stabilization, particularly in arid and semi arid zones	———

Priority 3

Grape	This includes wine, table, and raisin grapes. High priority is accorded to collection in China, the Himalayas, central Asia, southwestern Asia and the Mediterranean.

Priority S

Forage crops	———
Medicinal and drug plants	———

COUNTRY GROUPINGS

Fourteen regions are identified, although the developed countries of North America, Europe, and Oceania – other than the Mediterranean countries and the Soviet Republics of central Asia – are not included in these regions, even though many nations, institutes, and breeders in them are cooperating in the Board's work.

The grouping of countries into 14 regions is based largely on logistic considerations. Though it might be valuable to organize field programs on an ecological or phytogeographical basis, in practice, most regions include a range of ecological zones. Since exploration and collection will always be conducted by or in cooperation with national governments, the regions listed below consist of groups of adjacent nations sharing very broadly similar geographical situations.

The Mediterranean: Albania, Algeria, Cyprus, Egypt, France, Greece, Italy, Libya, Malta, Morocco, Portugal, Spain, Tunisia, and Yugoslavia

Southwestern Asia: Iraq, Israel, Jordan, Lebanon, Syria, Turkey, and the nations of the Arabian Peninsula

Central Asia: Afghanistan, Iran, Pakistan, and the Soviet Republics of central Asia

Southern Asia: Bangladesh, Bhutan, Burma, India, Nepal, and Sri Lanka

Southeast Asia: Indonesia, Malaysia, the Philippines, Papua, New Guinea, Thailand, and the nations of Indochina

Pacific Islands

East Asia: China, Japan, the Koreas, and Mongolia

Ethiopia

Eastern Africa: Botswana, Burundi, Kenya, Lesotho, Malawi, Madagascar, Mozambique, Ruanda, Somalia, Sudan, Swaziland, Tanzania, Uganda, Zambia, Zimbabwe, and the islands off eastern Africa

Western Africa: Angola, Benin, Cameroon, Central African Republic, Chad, Congo, Equatorial Guinea, Gabon, Gambia, Ghana, Guinea, Guinea-Bissau, Ivory Coast, Liberia, Mali, Mauritania, Niger, Nigeria, Senegal, Sierra Leone, the former Spanish Sahara, Togo, Upper Volta, and Zaire

Central America: Costa Rica, El Salvador, Guatemala, Honduras, Nicaragua, and Panama; Mexico, the Caribbean and the Guyanas

Brazil

Andean zone: Bolivia, Colombia, Ecuador, Peru, and Venezuela

Southern South America: Argentina, Chile, Paraguay, and Uruguay

REGIONAL PRIORITIES

Priority 1   The Mediterranean, southwestern Asia, central Asia, southern Asia, Ethiopia, Central America.

Priority 2   Southeast Asia, East Asia, West Africa, Brazil, the Andean zone.

Priority 3   Pacific Islands, eastern Africa, southern South America.

Abbreviations of Organizations

AVRDC	Asian Vegetable Research Development Center
CGIAR	Consultative Group on International Agricultural Research
CIAT	Centro Internacional de Agricultura Tropical (International Center for Tropical Agriculture)
CIP	Centro Internacional de la Papa (International Potato Center)
CIMMYT	Centro Internacional de Mejoramiento de Maiz y Trigo (International Maize and Wheat Improvement Center)
EUCARPIA	European Association for Research on Plant Breeding
FAO	Food and Agriculture Organization of the United Nations
IBP	International Biological Program
IBPGR	International Board for Plant Genetic Resources
ICARDA	International Center for Agricultural Research in the Dry Areas
ICRISAT	International Crops Research Institute for the Semi-Arid Tropics
IFPRI	International Food Policy Research Institute
IITA	International Institute of Tropical Agriculture
ILCA	International Livestock Center for Africa
ILRAD	International Laboratory for Research on Animal Diseases
IRRI	International Rice Research Institute
ISNAR	International Service for National Agricultural Research
IUBS	International Union of Biological Sciences
JIBP	Japanese International Biological Program
SABRAO	Society for the Advancement of Breeding Researches in Asia and Oceana
UNDP	United Nations Development Program
USDA	United States Department of Agriculture
WARDA	West Africa Rice Development Association

References

Alexander, D. E. 1975. The identification of high-quality protein variants and their use in crop plant improvement. In *Crop genetic resources for today and tomorrow*, ed. O. H. Frankel and J. G. Hawkes. IBP synthesis, vol. 2. Cambridge: Cambridge University Press.

Allard, R. W. 1970a. Population structure and sampling methods. In *Genetic resources in plants — their exploration and conservation*, ed. O. H. Frankel and E. Bennett. Oxford: Blackwell.

———— 1970b. Problems of maintenance. In *Genetic resources in plants — their exploration and conservation*, ed. O. H. Frankel and E. Bennett. Oxford: Blackwell.

Allard, R. W., A. L. Kahler, and B. S. Weir. 1971. Isozyme polymorphisms in barley populations. *Barley Genetics* 2:1–13.

Anderson, E. 1952. *Plants, man and life*. Berkeley: University of California Press.

———— 1960. The evolution of domestication. In *Evolution after Darwin*, ed. S. Tax and C. Callender. Chicago: University of Chicago Press.

Ashri, A. 1971. Evaluation of the world collection of safflower, *Carthamus tinctorius* L. I.: reaction to several diseases and associations with morphological characters in Israel. *Crop Science* 11:253–257.

Astley, D., and J. G. Hawkes. 1979. The nature of the Bolivian weed potato species *Solanum sucrense* Hawkes. *Euphytica* 28:685–696.

Ayers, A. D., J. W. Brown, and C. H. Wadleigh. 1952. Salt tolerance of barley and wheat in soil plots receiving several salinization regimes. *Agronomy Journal* 44:307–310.

Bajaj, Y. P. S. 1977. Clonal multiplication and cryopreservation of cassava through tissue culture. *Crop Improvement* 4:48–53.

Baker, H. G. 1970. Taxomony and the biological species concept in cultivated plants. In *Genetic resources in plants — their exploration and conservation*, ed. O. H. Frankel and E. Bennett. Oxford: Blackwell.

Bell, G. D. H. 1965. The comparative phylogeny of the temperate cereals.

In *Essays on crop plant evolution,* ed. J. Hutchinson. Cambridge: Cambridge University Press.

Bennett, E., ed. 1968. *Record of the FAO/IBP technical conference on the exploration, utilization and conservation of plant genetic resources.* Rome:FAO.

_____1970a. Adaptation in wild and cultivated plant populations. In *Genetic resources in plants — their exploration and conservation,* ed. O.H. Frankel and E. Bennett. Oxford: Blackwell.

_____1970b. Tactics of plant exploration. In *Genetic resources in plants — their exploration and conservation,* ed. O. H. Frankel and E. Bennett. Oxford: Blackwell.

_____1971. The origin and importance of agroecotypes in south-west Asia. In *Plant life of south-west Asia,* ed. P. H. Davis, P. C. Harper, and I. C. Hedge. Edinburgh: Botanical Society of Edinburgh.

_____1973. In *Survey of crop genetic resources in their centres of diversity: first report,* ed. O. H. Frankel. Rome: FAO/IBP.

Bradshaw, A. D. 1975. Population structure and the effects of isolation and selection. In *Crop genetic resources for today and tomorrow,* ed. O. H. Frankel and J. G. Hawkes. IBP synthesis, vol. 2. Cambridge: Cambridge University Press.

Braidwood, R. J. 1960. The agricultural revolution. *Scientific American,* 203: 130-148.

Bray, W. 1976. From predation to production: the nature of agricultural evolution in Mexico and Peru. In *Problems in economic and social archaeology,* ed. G. G. Sieveking, I. H. Longworth, and K. E. Wilson. London: Duckworth.

Bray, W. 1977. From foraging to farming in early Mexico. In *Hunters, gatherers and first farmers beyond Europe: an archaeological survey,* ed. J. V. S. Megaw. Leicester: Leicester University Press.

Brezhnev. D. 1970. Mobilization, conservation and utilization of plant resources at the N. I. Vavilov All-Union Institute of Plant Industry, Leningrad. In *Genetic resources in plants — their exploration and conservation,* ed. O. H. Frankel and E. Bennett. Oxford: Blackwell.

_____1975. Plant exploration in the USSR. In *Crop genetic resources for today and tomorrow,* ed. O. H. Frankel and J. G. Hawkes. IBP synthesis, vol. 2. Cambridge: Cambridge University Press.

Brothwell, D., and P. Brothwell. 1969. *Food in antiquity.* London: Thames and Hudson.

Brown, A., E. Nevo, and D. Zohary. 1977. Association of alleles at esterase loci in wild barley *Hordeum spontaneum* L. *Nature* (London) 268:430–431.

Brücher, H. 1969. Gibt es Gen-Zentren? *Naturwissenschaften* 56:77–84.

Bunting, A. H. 1960. Some reflections on the ecology of weeds. In *The biology of weeds,* ed. J. L. Harper. Oxford: Blackwell.

Burkart, A., and H. Brücher. 1953. *Phaseolus aborigineus* Burkart Mutmassliche andine Stammform der Kulturbohne. *Der Züchter* 23:65–72.

Candolle, A. de. 1855. *Géographie botanique raisonnée.* Paris.
_____1882. *Origine des plantes cultivées.* Paris (English translation, 1886, Kegan Paul).
CGIAR 1974. *International research in agriculture.* New York: CGIAR.
_____1976. *The Consultative Group on International Agricultural Research.* New York: UNDP.
Chang, K. C. 1970. The beginnings of agriculture in the Far East. *Antiquity* 44: 175–185.
Chang, T. T., G. C. Loresto, and O. Tagumpay. 1974. Screening rice germ plasm for drought resistance. *SABRAO Journal.* 6:9–16.
Chang, T. T., S. H. Ou, M. D. Pathak, K. C. Ling, and H. E. Kauffman. 1975. The search for disease and insect resistance in rice germplasm. In *Crop genetic resources for today and tomorrow,* ed. O. H. Frankel and J. G. Hawkes. IBP synthesis, vol. 2. Cambridge: Cambridge University Press.
Childe, V. G. 1936. *Man makes himself.* London: Watts.
Chin, H. F., and E. H. Roberts. 1980. *Recalcitrant crop seeds.* Kuala Lumpur: Tropical Press.
CIMMYT Today. 1977. Turkey's wheat research and training project. *Report No. 6.* Mexico: CIMMYT.
CIP. 1973. *Workshop on germ-plasm exploration and taxonomy of potatoes: I.* Lima, Peru: CIP.
_____1976. *Planning conference report – exploration and maintenance of germplasm resources: II.* Lima, Peru: CIP.
_____1979. *Planning conference report – exploration, taxonomy and maintenance of potato germplasm: III.* Lima, Peru: CIP.
Cooper, J. P. 1970. Environmental physiology. In *Genetic resources in plants – their exploration and conservation,* ed. O. H. Frankel and E. Bennett. Oxford: Blackwell.
Cribb, P. J. 1972. Studies on the origin of *Solanum tuberosum* L. subsp. *andigena* (Juz. et Buk.) Hawkes – the cultivated tetraploid potato of South America. Ph.D. thesis, University of Birmingham (England).

D'Amato, F. 1975. The problem of genetic stability in plant tissue and cell cultures. In *Crop genetic resources for today and tomorrow,* ed. O. H. Frankel and J. G. Hawkes. IBP synthesis, vol. 2. Cambridge: Cambridge University Press.
Darlington, C. D. and Janaki Ammal, E. K. 1945. *Chromosome Atlas of Cultivated Plants.* London: Allen & Unwin
Darlington, C. D. 1956, 1963, 1973. *Chromosome botany and the origins of cultivated plants,* 1st, 2d, and 3d eds. London: Allen & Unwin.
Darwin, C. 1868. *The variation of animals and plants under domestication.* London.
Dearborn, C. H. 1969. Alaska Frostless, an inherently frost resistant potato variety. *American Potato Journal* 46:1–4.
Denton, I. R., R. J. Westcott, and B. V. Ford-Lloyd. 1977. Phenotypic variation of *Solanum tuberosum* cv. Dr. McIntosh regenerated directly from

shoot-tip culture. *Potato Research* 20:131–136.

Dinoor, A. 1975. Evaluation of sources of disease resistance. In *Crop genetic resources for today and tomorrow,* ed. O. H. Frankel and J. G. Hawkes. IBP synthesis, vol. 2. Cambridge: Cambridge University Press.

Dionne, L. A. 1961. Mechanisms of interspecific incompatibility in tuber-bearing *Solanum* species. *American Potato Journal* 38:73–77.

———1963. Studies on the use of *Solanum acaule* as a bridge between *Solanum tuberosum* and species in the series Bulbocastana, Cardiophylla, and Pinnatisecta. *Euphytica* 12: 263–269.

Doggett, H. 1965. The development of the cultivated sorghums. In *Essays on crop plant evolution,* ed. J. Hutchinson. Cambridge: Cambridge University Press.

Dorofeev, V. F. 1975. Evaluation of material for frost and drought resistance in wheat breeding. In *Crop genetic resources for today and tomorrow,* ed. O. H. Frankel and J. G. Hawkes. IBP synthesis, vol. 2. Cambridge: Cambridge University Press

Edwards, C. A. 1981. Potential storage life of *Citrus aurantiaca* L. seeds. Ph.D. thesis, University of Birmingham (England).

Engel, F. 1970. Exploration of the Chilca Canyon, Peru. *Current Anthropology* 11:55–58.

Englebrecht, T. H. 1916. Über die Entstehung einiger feldmässig angebauter Kulturpflanzen. *Geographische Zeitschrift* 22:328–335.

FAO 1961. *FAO technical meeting on plant exploration and introduction.* Rome: FAO.

———1967. *Report of the FAO/IBP technical conference on the exploration, utilization and conservation of plant genetic resources.* Rome: FAO.

———1968. *Report of the first session of the FAO Panel of Experts on Forest Gene Resources.* Rome: FAO.

———1969. *Report of the third session of the FAO Panel of Experts on Plant Exploration and Introduction.* Rome: FAO.

———1970. *Report of the fourth session of the FAO Panel of Experts on Plant Exploration and Introduction.* Rome: FAO.

———1973. *Report of the fifth session of the FAO Panel of Experts on Plant Exploration and Introduction.* Rome: FAO.

———1974. *Report of the sixth session of the FAO Panel of Experts on Plant Exploration and Introduction.* Rome: FAO.

Flannery, K. V. 1973. The origins of agriculture. In *Annual Review of Anthropology,* vol. 2, ed. B. J. Siegel, A. R. Beals, and S. A. Tyler. 1973:271–310.

Ford-Lloyd, B. V. 1978. Data storage and retrieval systems in genetic resources information exchange. In *Conservation of plant genetic resources: proceedings of Section K, jointly with Section M of the British Association for the Advancement of Science, Aston 1977,* ed. J. G. Hughes. Birmingham: University of Aston in Birmingham (England).

Frankel, O. H. 1970a. Save the genetic treasuries in the SABRAO region. SA-
BRAO Newsletter 2:1–6.

_____1970b. Genetic dangers in the green revolution. *World Agriculture*
19:9–14.

_____1972. Genetic conservation – a parable of the scientist's social re-
sponsibility. *Search* 3:193–201.

_____ed. 1973. *Survey of crop genetic resources in their centres of diversity:
first report.* Rome: FAO/IBP.

_____1974. Genetic conservation – our evolutionary responsibility. *Gene-
tics* 78:53–65.

Frankel, O. H., and E. Bennett, eds. 1970. *Genetic resources in plants – their
exploration and conservation.* Oxford: Blackwell.

Frankel, O. H., and J. G. Hawkes, eds. 1975. *Crop genetic resources for today
and tomorrow.* IBP synthesis, vol. 2. Cambridge: Cambridge University
Press.

Frankel, O. H., E. H. Roberts, and J. G. Hawkes. 1974. *Proposed standards
and procedures for seed storage installations used for long-term conservation of base collections: report of the sixth session of the FAO
Panel of Experts on Plant Exploration and Introduction.* Rome: FAO.

Frankel, O. H., and M. E. Soulé. 1981. *Conservation and evolution.* Cambridge: Cambridge University Press.

Fröst, S., G. Holm, and S. Asker. 1975. *Flavonoid patterns and the phylogeny
of barley. Hereditas* 79:133–142.

Glob, P. V. 1969. *The Bog People.* London: Paladin.

Gorman, C. F. 1969. Hoabinthian: a pebble tool complex with early plant associations in south-east Asia. *Science* 163:671–673.

Grant, W. F. 1967. Cytogenetic factors associated with the evolution of
weeds. *Taxon* 16:283–293.

Grout, B. W. W., and G. G. Henshaw. 1978. Freeze preservation of potato
shoot-tip cultures. *Annals of Botany* 42:1227–1229.

_____1980. Growth of potato shoot-tip cultures after storage in liquid nitro-
gen. *Annals of Botany* 46:243–248.

Grout, B. W. W., R. J. Westcott, and G. G. Henshaw. 1977. Scanning electron
microscope studies of multiple shoot production by meristem tip cultures of *Solanum* x *curtilobum. Annals of Botany* 41:1113–1116.

Harlan, H. V., and M. L. Martini. 1936. Problems and results in barley breeding. *USDA Yearbook of Agriculture,* 1936:303–346.

Harlan, J. R. 1951. Anatomy of gene centers. *American Naturalist* 85:97–103.

_____1965. The possible role of weed races in the evolution of cultivated
plants. *Euphytica* 14:173–176.

_____1970. Evolution of cultivated plants. In *Genetic resources in plants –
their exploration and conservation,* ed. O. H. Frankel and E. Bennett.
Oxford: Blackwell.

_____1971. Agricultural origins: centers and noncenters. *Science 174:468–*

474.

_____1972. Genetics of disaster. *Journal of Environmental Quality* 1:212–215.

_____1975a. Our vanishing genetic resources. *Science* 188:618–621.

_____1975b. Seed crops. In *Crop genetic resources for today and tomorrow*, ed. O. H. Frankel and J. G. Hawkes. IBP synthesis, vol. 2. Cambridge: Cambridge University Press.

_____1975c. *Crops and man.* Madison, Wisconsin: American Society of Agronomy, and Crop Science Society of America.

_____1975d. Geographic patterns of variation in some cultivated plants. *Journal of Heredity* 66:184–191.

_____1976. Genetic resources in wild relatives of crops. *Crop Science* 16: 329–333.

Harlan, J. R., and J. M. J. de Wet. 1965. Some thoughts about weeds. *Economic Botany* 19:16–24.

Harlan, J. R., J. M. J. de Wet, and E. G. Price. 1973. Comparative evolution of cereals. *Evolution* 27:311–325.

Harrington, J. F. 1970. Seed and pollen storage for conservation of plant gene resources. In *Genetic resources in plants — their exploration and conservation,* ed. O. H. Frankel and E. Bennett. Oxford: Blackwell.

Harris, D. R. 1967. New light on plant domestication and the origins of agriculture: a review. *Geographical Review* 57:90–107.

_____1969. Agricultural systems, ecosystems and the origins of agriculture. In *The domestication and exploration of plants and animals,* ed. P. J. Ucko and G. W. Dimbleby. London: Duckworth

_____1973. The prehistory of tropical agriculture: an ethno-ecological model. In *The explanation of culture change,* ed. C. Renfrew. London: Duckworth.

_____1978. The environmental impact of traditional and modern agricultural systems. In *Conservation and agriculture,* ed. J. G. Hawkes. London: Duckworth.

Hartley, W. 1970. Climate and crop distribution. In *Genetic resources in plants — their exploration and conservation,* ed. O. H. Frankel and F Bennett. Oxford. Blackwell.

Hawkes, J. G. 1958. Significance of wild species and primitive forms for potato breeding. *Euphytica* 7:257–270.

_____1962. The origin of *Solanum juzepczukii* Buk. and *S. curtilobum* Juz. et Buk.. *Zeitschrift für Pflanzenzüchtung* 47:1–14.

_____1969. The ecological background of plant domestication. In *The domestication and exploitation of plants and animals,* ed. P. J. Ucko and G. W. Dimbleby. London: Duckworth.

_____1971. Conservation of plant genetic resources. *Outlook on agriculture* 6:248–253.

_____1975. Vegetatively propagated crops. In *Crop genetic resources for today and tomorrow,* ed. O. H. Frankel and J. G. Hawkes. IBP synthesis, vol. 2. Cambridge: Cambridge University Press.

_____1976. Sampling gene pools. In *Conservation of threatened plants,* ed. J. B. Simmons, R. I. Beyer, P. E. Brandham, G. L. Lucas, and V. T. H. Parry. New York and London: Plenum Press.

_____1977a. The importance of wild germplasm in plant breeding. *Euphytica* 26:615–621.

_____1977b. The taxonomist's role in the conservation of genetic diversity. In *Essays in plant taxonomy,* ed. H. E. Street. London: Academic Press.

_____ed. 1978. *Conservation and agriculture.* London: Duckworth.

_____1980. *Crop genetic resources field collection manual.* Wageningen, The Netherlands: IBPGR/EUCARPIA.

_____1981. Germplasm collection, preservation and use. In *Plant breeding II,* ed. K. V. Frey. Ames, Iowa: Iowa State University Press.

_____1982. Genetic conservation of "recalcitrant species – an overview. In *Crop genetic resources: the conservation of difficult material,* ed. L. Withers. Paris: IUBS/IBPGR.

Hawkes, J. G., and H. Lamberts. 1977. Eucarpia's fifteen years of activities in genetic resources. *Euphytica* 26:1–3.

Hawkes, J. G., and J. T. Williams. 1976. The first six years: postgraduate training at Birmingham. *Plant Genetic Resources Newsletter* 32:2–7.

Hawkes, J. G., J. T. Williams, and J. Hanson. 1976. *A bibliography of plant genetic resources.* Rome: IBPGR.

Hegnauer, R. 1975. Secondary metabolites and crop plants. In *Crop genetic resources for today and tomorrow,* ed. O. H. Frankel and J. G. Hawkes. IBP synthesis, vol. 2. Cambridge: Cambridge University Press.

Heiser, C. B. 1955. The origin and development of the cultivated sunflower. *American Biology Teacher,* May 1955:161–167.

_____1973. *Seed to civilization: the story of man's food.* San Francisco: W. H. Freeman.

Henshaw, G. G. 1975. Technical aspects of tissue culture storage for genetic conservation. In *Crop genetic resources for today and tomorrow,* ed. O. H. Frankel and J. G. Hawkes. IBP synthesis, vol. 2. Cambridge: Cambridge University Press.

_____1979. Plant tissue culture: its potential for dissemination of pathogen-free germplasm and multiplication of planting material. In *Plant health,* ed. D. L. Ebbels and J. E. King. Oxford: Blackwell.

Henshaw, G. G., J. A. Stamp, and R. J. Westcott. 1980. Tissue cultures and germplasm storage. In *Plant cell cultures: results and perspectives,* ed. F. Sala, B. Parisi, R. Cella, and O. Ciferri. Amsterdam and Oxford: Elsevier / North-Holland Biomedical Press.

Henshaw, G. G., J. F. O'Hara, and R. J. Westcott. 1980. Tissue culture methods for the storage and utilization of potato germplasm. In *Tissue culture methods for plant pathologists,* ed. D. S. Ingram and J. P. Helgeson. Oxford: Blackwell.

Hersh, G. N., and D. J. Rogers. 1975. Documentation and information requirements for genetic resources application. In *Crop genetic resources for today and tomorrow,* ed. O. H. Frankel and J. G. Hawkes. IBP synthesis, vol. 2. Cambridge: Cambridge University Press.

Humboldt, A. von 1807. *Essai sur la géographie des plantes.* Paris.

Hutchinson, J., ed. 1965. *Essays on crop plant evolution.* Cambridge: Cambridge University Press.

Hutchinson, J. B. 1978. The Indian achievement. In *Conservation and agriculture,* ed. J. G. Hawkes. London: Duckworth.

Hyland, H. L. 1970. Description and evaluation of wild and primitive introduced plants. In *Genetic resources in plants — their exploration and conservation,* ed. O. H. Frankel and E. Bennett. Oxford: Blackwell.

_____1975. Recent plant exploration in the USA. In *Crop genetic resources for today and tomorrow,* ed. O. H. Frankel and J. G. Hawkes. IBP synthesis, vol. 2. Cambridge: Cambridge University Press.

IBPGR. 1974. *Report of the first meeting, Rome, 5-7 June 1974.* Rome: CGIAR.

_____1975. *Programme and budget proposals for 1976.* Rome: CGIAR.

_____1976a. *News bulletin of current activities.* Rome: IBPGR.

_____1976b. *Advisory Committee on the Genetic Resources Communication, Information and Documentation System (GR/CIDS), first report.* Rome: IBPGR.

_____1976c. *Report of IBPGR working group on engineering, design and cost aspects of long-term seed storage facilities.* Rome: IBPGR.

_____1981a. *Crop genetic resources.* Rome: IBPGR.

_____1981b. *Revised priorities among crops and regions.* Rome: FAO, IBPGR Executive Secretariat.

_____1981c. *Genetic resources of Cruciferous crops.* Rome: IBPGR Secretariat.

Innes, N. L. 1975. Genetic conservation and the breeding of field vegetables for the United Kingdom. *Outlook on Agriculture* 8:301–305.

Jain, S. K. 1975. Population structure and the effects of breeding system. In *Crop genetic resources for today and tomorrow,* ed. O. H. Frankel and J. G. Hawkes. IBP synthesis, vol. 2. Cambridge: Cambridge University Press.

Jain, S. K., C. O. Qualset, G. M. Bhatt, and K. K. Wu. 1975. Geographical patterns of phenotypic diversity in a world collection of *durum* wheats. *Crop Science* 15:700–704.

Jawahar, Ram, and D. V. S. Panwar. 1970. Intraspecific divergence in rice. *Indian Journal of Genetics and Plant Breeding* 30:1–10.

Jeswani, L. M., B. R. Murty, and R. B. Mehra. 1970. Divergence in relation to geographical origin in a world collection of linseed. *Indian Journal of Genetics and Plant Breeding.* 30:11–25.

Julen, G., and S. Ellerstrom. 1973. The need for genetic conservation. In *European and regional gene banks,* ed. J. G. Hawkes and W. Lange. Wageningen: EUCARPIA.

Kaplan, L. 1965. Archaeology and domestication in American *Phaseolus* (beans). *Economic Botany* 19:358–368.

Kaplan, L., T. F. Lynch, and C. E. Smith. 1973. Early cultivated beans *(Phaseolus vulgaris)* from an intermontane Peruvian valley. *Science* 179:76–77.

Kimber, C. T. 1973. Spatial patterning in the dooryard gardens of Puerto Rico. *Geographical Review* 63:6–26.

Konzak, C. F. 1973. Standardized documentation procedures for germ plasm collection. In *European and regional gene banks,* ed. J. G. Hawkes and W. Lange. Wageningen: EUCARPIA.

Kuckuck, H. 1962. Vavilov's Genzentrentheorie in heutiger Sicht. *Third Congress of EUCARPIA.* 1962:177–196.

Kupzov, A. I. 1959. Parallelism in the variability of plant species with certain common characters. *Zeitschrift für Pflanzenzüchtung* 41:313–325.

_____1965. The formation of areas of cultivated plants. *Zeitschrift für Pflanzenzüchtung* 53:53–66.

_____1976. Basic loci in cultivation of certain crops in the past and in modern times. *Theoretical and Applied Genetics* 18:209–215.

McNeish, R. S. 1964. Ancient Mesoamerican civilization. *Science* 143:531–537.

_____1965. The origins of American agriculture. *Antiquity* 39:87–94.

_____1972. The evolution of community patterns in the Tehuacán Valley of Mexico and speculations about the cultural processes. In *Man, settlement and urbanism,* ed. P. J. Ucko, R. Tringham, and G. W. Dimbleby. London: Duckworth.

Mangelsdorf, P. C. 1965. Genetics, agriculture, and the world food problem. *Proceedings of the American Philosophical Society* 109:242–248.

Mangelsdorf, P. C., R. S. MacNeish, and W. C. Galinat. 1967. Prehistoric wild and cultivated maize. In *Prehistory of the Tehuacán Valley,* vol. 1, ed. D. S. Byers. Austin, Texas, and London: University of Texas Press.

Mangelsdorf, P. C., R. S. MacNeish, and G. R. Willey. 1964. Origins of agriculture in Middle America. In *Handbook of Middle American Indians, 1. Natural environment and early cultures,* ed. R. Wauchope. Austin, Texas: University of Texas Press.

Marshall, D. R., and A. H. D. Brown. 1975. Optimum sampling strategies in genetic conservation. In *Crop genetic resources for today and tomorrow,* ed. O. H. Frankel and J. G. Hawkes. IBP synthesis, vol. 2. Cambridge: Cambridge University Press.

Martins, R. 1976. New archaeological techniques for the study of ancient root crops in Peru. Ph.D. thesis, University of Birmingham (England).

Matsuo, T., ed. 1975. *Gene conservation — exploration, collection, preservation and utilization of genetic resources.* JIBP synthesis, vol. 5. Tokyo: University of Tokyo Press.

Morel, G. 1975. Meristem culture techniques for the long-term storage of cultivated plants. In *Crop genetic resources for today and tomorrow,* ed.

O. H. Frankel and J. G. Hawkes. IBP synthesis, vol. 2. Cambridge: Cambridge University Press.

Moseley, M. E. 1972. Subsistence and demography: an example of interaction from prehistoric Peru. *South West Journal of Anthropology* 28:25–49.

Mumford, P. M., and B. W. W. Grout. 1978. Germination and liquid nitrogen storage of cassava seed. *Annals of Botany* 42:255–257.

———1979. Dessication and low temperature (−196°C) tolerance of *Citrus limon* seed. *Seed Science and Technology* 7:407–410.

Müntzing, A. 1966. On the evolution and breeding of cultivated plants. *Indian Journal of Genetics* 26:3–13.

Murra, J. V. 1972. El control vertical de un máximo de pisos ecológicos en la economía de las sociedades Andinas. *Visita a la Provincia de León de Huánuco por Iñigo Ortiz* 2:429–476.

Nakagahra, M., T. Akihama, and K. Hayashi. 1975. Genetic variation and geographic cline of esterase isozymes in native rice varieties. *Japanese Journal of Genetics* 50:373–382.

National Academy of Sciences. 1972. *Genetic vulnerability of major crops.* Washington, D.C. National Academy of Sciences.

———1975. *Underexploited tropical plants with promising economic value.* Washington, D.C. National Academy of Sciences.

Nevo, E., A. Brown, and D. Zohary. 1979. Genetic diversity in the wild progenitor of barley in Israel. *Experientia* 35:1027–1029.

Ng, N. Q., T. T. Chang, J. T. Williams, and J. G. Hawkes. 1981. Morphological studies of Asian rice and its related wild species and the recognition of a new Australian taxon. *Biological Journal of the Linnean Society* 16: 303–313.

Payne, P. 1974. Protein deficiency or starvation? *New Scientist,* November 1974:393–396.

Pickersgill, B., and C. B. Heiser. 1976. Cytogenetics and evolutionary change under domestication. *Philosophical Transactions of the Royal Society of London B.* 275:55–69.

Ping-Ti Ho. 1969. The loess and the origin of Chinese agriculture. *American Historical Review* 75:1–36.

———1976. *The cradle of the East: an inquiry into the indigenous origins of techniques and ideas of Neolithic and Early Historic China, 5000–1000 B.C.* Chicago: Chinese University of Hong Kong. University of Chicago Press.

Porceddu, E. 1976. Variation for agronomical traits in a world collection of durum wheat. *Zeitschrift für Pflanzenzüchtung* 77:314–329.

Portères, R. 1950. Vieilles agricultures africaines avant le XVIème siècle. *L'Agronomie Tropicale* 5:489:–507.

Portères, R. 1962. Berceaux agricoles primaires sur le continent africain. *Journal of African History* 3:195:210.

Prana, M. S. 1977. Studies on some Indonesian *Curcuma* species. Ph.D. thesis, University of Birmingham (England).

Prescott-Allen, R., and C. Prestcott-Allen, 1981. In situ conservation of crop genetic resources. Report to IBPGR, Rome (Mimeographed).

Qualset, C. O. 1975. Sampling germplasm in a center of diversity: an example of disease resistance in Ethiopian barley. In *Crop genetic resources for today and tomorrow*, ed. O. H. Frankel and J. G. Hawkes. IBP synthesis, vol. 2. Cambridge: University of Cambridge.

Renfrew, J. M. 1973. *Palaeoethnobotany*. London: Methuen.

Richardson, D. G., and N. Estrada Ramos. 1971. Evaluation of frost resistant tuber-bearing *Solanum* hybrids. *American Potato Journal* 48:339–343.

Rick, C. M. 1967. Exploiting species hybrids for vegetable improvement. *Proceedings of the XVII International Horticultural Congress, vol. 3.* 1976:217–229.

Riley, R., and V. Chapman. 1958. Genetic control of the cytologically diploid behaviour of hexaploid wheat. *Nature* (London) 182:713–715.

Röbbelen, G. 1975. Screening for oils and fats in plants. In *Crop genetic resources for today and tomorrow*, ed. O. H. Frankel and J. G. Hawkes. IBP synthesis, vol. 2. Cambridge: Cambridge University Press.

Roberts, E. H. 1973. Predicting the storage life of seeds. *Seed Science and Technology* 1:499:514.

————1974. Recommended conditions for seed storage at genetic resources centres. *Report of the sixth session of the FAO Panel of Experts on Plant Exploration and Introduction.* Rome: FAO.

————1975. Problems of long-term storage of seed and pollen for genetic resources conservation. In *Crop genetic resources for today and tomorrow*, ed. O. H. Frankel and J. G. Hawkes. IBP synthesis, vol. 2. Cambridge: Cambridge University Press.

Rogers, D. J., B. Snoad, and L. Seidewitz. 1975. Documentation for genetic resources centers. In *Crop genetic resources for today and tomorrow*, ed. O. H. Frankel and J. G. Hawkes. IBP synthesis, vol. 2. Cambridge: Cambridge University Press.

Ross, R. W., and P. R. Rowe. 1969. Utilizing the frost resistance of diploid *Solanum* species. *American Potato Journal* 46:5–13.

Rowe, P. R., and L. Sequeira. 1970. Inheritance of resistance to *Pseudomonas solanacearum* in *Solanum phureja*. *Phytopathology* 60:1499:–1501.

Sakai, A., and M. Noshiro. 1975. Some factors contributing to the survival of crop seeds cooled to the temperature of liquid nitrogen. In *Crop genetic resources for today and tomorrow*, ed. O. H. Frankel and J. G. Hawkes. IBP synthesis, vol. 2. Cambridge: Cambridge University Press.

Sakamura, T. 1918. Kurtze Mitteilung über die Chromosomenzahlen und die Verwandtschaftsverhältnisse der *Triticum*. *Botanical Magazine, Tokyo* 32:151–154.

Sauer, C. O. 1952. *Agricultural origins and dispersals.* New York: American Geographical Society.

———1969. *Agricultural origins and dispersals.* Cambridge, Mass.: Massachusetts Institute of Technology Press.

Schiemann, E. 1930. Gedenken zur Genzentrentheorie Vavilovs. *Naturwissenschaften* 27:377–383, 394–401.

———1943. Entstehung der Kulturpflanzen. *Ergebnisse der Biologie* 19: 409–551.

———1951. New results on the history of cultivated cereals. *Heredity* 5: 305–320.

Schwanitz, F. 1967. *Die Evolution der Kulturpflanzen.* Munich, Basel, and Vienna: Bayerischer Landwirtschaftsverlag.

Seibert, M. 1976. Shoot initiation from carnation shoot apices frozen to 196° C. *Science* 191:1178–1179.

Smartt, J. 1969. The evolution of American *Phaseolus* beans under domestication. In *The domestication and exploitation of plants and animals,* ed. P. J. Ucko and G. W. Dimbleby. London: Duckworth.

———1976. *Tropical pulses.* London: Longman.

Solbrig, O. T. 1970. *Principles and methods of plant biosystematics.* Toronto: Macmillan.

Sprague, E. W., and K. W. Finlay. 1976. Current status of plant resources and utilization. Paper presented at World Food Conference. *CIMMYT Translations and Reprints,* no. 19.

Stamp. J. A. 1978. Freeze preservation of shoot-tips of potato varieties. M.Sc. thesis, University of Birmingham (England).

Stebbins, G. L. 1950. *Variation and evolution in plants.* New York: Columbia University Press.

Stebbins, G. L., and D. Zohary. 1959. Cytogenetic and evolutionary studies in the genus *Dactylis:* I. *University of California Publications in Botany* 31:1–40.

Stegemann, H., and V. Loeshcke. 1976. Index of European potato varieties. *Mitteilungen aus der Biologischen Bundesanstalt für Land-und Fortwirtschaft, Berlin Dahlem* 168:1–215.

Swaminathan, M. S. 1954. Microsporogenesis in some commercial potato varieties. *Journal of Heredity* 45:205–272.

———1970. The significance of polyploidy in the origin of species and species groups. In *Genetic resources in plants — their exploration and conservation,* ed. O. H. Frankel and E. Benett. Oxford: Blackwell.

Sykes, J. T. 1975. Tree crops. In *Crop genetic resources for today and tomorrow,* ed. O. H. Frankel and J. G. Hawkes. IBP synthesis, vol. 2. Cambridge: Cambridge University Press.

Tahir, M., and I. Hussain. 1975. Salt tolerance studies in rice. *Agriculture, Pakistan* 26:125–135.

Thurston, H. D., and T. J. C. Lozano. 1968. Resistance to bacterial wilt of potatoes in Colombian clones of *Solanum phureja. American Potato Journal* 45:51–55.

Ucko, P. J., and G. W. Dimbleby, eds. 1969. *The domestication and exploitation of plants and animals.* London: Duckworth.

Udovenko, G. V. 1975. Salt-tolerance in cultivated plants and its physiological nature. *Bulletin of Applied Botany, Genetics and Plant Breeding* 54: 173–187. In Russian.

Van der Plank, J. E. 1968. *Disease resistance in plants.* New York: Academic Press.

Van Zeist, W. 1970. The Oriental Institute excavations at Mureybit, Syria: preliminary report on the 1965 campaign; part III: the paleobotany. *Journel of Near Eastern Studies* 29:167–176.

Van Zeist, W., and W. A. Casparie. 1968. Wild einkorn wheat and barley from Tell Mureybit in northern Syria. *Acta Botanica Neerlandica* 17: 44–53.

Vavilov, N. I. 1922. The law of homologous series in variation. *Journal of Genetics* 12:47–90.

_____1926. Studies on the origin of cultivated plants. *Bulletin of Applied Botany, Genetics and Plant Breeding* 16: 1–248. In Russian.

_____1930. Wild progenitors of the fruit trees of Turkistan and the Caucasus and the problem of the origin of fruit trees. *Proceedings of the IX International Horticultural Congress, Group B.* 1930:271–286.

_____ed. 1935. *Theoretical bases of plant breeding, vol. 2. Special part: grain and forage crops.* Moscow and Leningrad. In Russian.

_____ed. 1937. *Theoretical bases of plant breeding, vol. 3.* Moscow and Leningrad. In Russian.

_____1940. The new systematics of cultivated plants. In *The new systematics,* ed. J. Huxley. Oxford: Clarendon Press.

_____1951. The origin, variation, immunity and breeding of cultivated plants. *Chronica Botanica* 13:1–366. (Translated from Russian by K. Starr Chester.)

_____1957. Published in English in 1960. *World resources of cereals, leguminous seed crops and flax, and their utilization in plant breeding.* Jerusalem: Israel Program for Scientific Translations.

Villiers, T. A. 1975. Genetic maintenance of seeds in imbibed storage. In *Crop genetic resources for today and tomorrow,* ed. O. H. Frankel and J. G. Hawkes. IBP synthesis, vol. 2. Cambridge: Cambridge University Press.

Westcott, R. J., G. G. Henshaw, B. W. W. Grout, and W. M. Roca. 1977. Tissue culture methods and germplasm storage in potato. *Acta Horticulturae* 78:45–49.

Whitmore, T. C. 1975. *Tropical rain forests of the Far East.* Oxford: Clarendon Press.

Whyte, R. O. 1958. Plant exploration, collection and introduction. *FAO Agri-*

cultural Studies no. 41. Rome: FAO.

Wilkes, H. G. 1967. *Teosinte: the closest relative of maize*. Cambridge, Mass.: Bussey Institution, Harvard University.

Williams, J. T. 1976. *A bibliography of plant genetic resources — supplement*. Rome: IBPGR.

Williams, J. T., C. H. Lamoureux, and N. Wulijarni-Soetjipto, eds. 1975. *South East Asian plant genetic resources*. Bogor, Indonesia.

Willis, J. C. 1922. *Age and area*. Cambridge: Cambridge Univerisity Press.

Witcombe, J. R. 1975. Bangor Lyallpur Universities expedition to Northern Pakistan, 1974. *Genetic Conservation Report*. Bangor, Wales: School of Plant Biology, Bangor University.

Witcombe, J. R., and M. M. Gilani. 1979. Variation in cereals from the Himalayas and the optimum strategy for sampling plant germplasm. *Journal of Applied Ecology* 16:633–640.

Witcombe, J. R., and A. R. Rao. 1976. The genecology of wheat in a Nepalese centre of diversity. *Journal of Applied Ecology* 13:915–924.

Yen, D. E. 1967. The economic aspects of the Pacific sweet potato collection. In *Proceedings of the First International Symposium on Tropical Root Crops*, vol. 1. St. Augustine, Trinidad: University of the West Indies.

Zeven, A. C. 1973. Dr. Th. H. Engelbrecht's views on the origin of cultivated plants. *Euphytica* 22:279–287.

Zhukovsky, P. M. 1970. The world gene pool of plants for breeding (mega-gene-centers and micro-gene-centers). In *N. I. Vavilov and agricultural science*. Moscow. (In Russlan.)

———1975. *World gene pool of plants for breeding. Mega-genecenters and endemic micro genecenters*. Leningrad: USSR Academy of Sciences

Zohary, D. 1969. The progenitors of wheat and barley in relation to domestication and agricultural dispersal in the Old World. In *The domestication and exploitation of plants and animals*, ed. P. J. Ucko and G. W. Dimbleby. London: Duckworth.

———1970. Centers of diversity and centers of origin. In *Genetic resources in plants — their exploration and conservation*, ed. O. H. Frankel and E. Bennett. Oxford: Blackwell.

———1973. The origin of cultivated cereals and pulses in the Near East. In *Chromosones today*, vol. 4., ed. J. Wahrman and K. R. Lewis. New York: Wiley.

Zohary, D., and M. Hopf. 1973. Domestication of pulses in the Old World. *Science* 182:887–894.

Index